An Introduction to

Irish Ancestry

Seán E. Quinn
B.A. (Hons.), H. Dip. in Ed., M. Litt., Barrister-at-Law.

Third Edition

Irish Genealogy Press
2002

Published in 2002 by Irish Genealogy Press,
15 Rathclaren, Killarney, Bray, Co. Wicklow, Ireland.

First Edition   1990
Second Edition   2000

Cataloguing In Publication Data for Libraries

Quinn, Seán Eoghan

An Introduction to Irish Ancestry

929.19415   CS 483 Q85

ISBN 1 871509 44 0 Pck

© Seán E. Quinn 2002

The Moral Rights of Seán E. Quinn to be identified as author of
this work has been asserted by him in accordance with
the Copyright and Related Rights Act, 2000.

Cover: Hannah McLaughlin (nee Barr), author's maternal grandmother
Clonglash 1950.

Printed by Johnswood Press Ltd., Airton Business Park, Dublin 24, Ireland.

Preface

The purpose of this book is to help you trace your Irish Ancestors. In the main the book deals with the two principal aspects that there are to researching your family tree: the records and the repositories in which those records are held.

A glance at the contents will show the five basic records, and the principal repositories in which they are held. These basic records will help you trace your ancestors back to the late eighteenth or early nineteenth century. It is my own belief based upon thirty-five years of genealogical research, that the majority of Irish people are most unlikely to be able to trace their ancestors back further than the late eighteenth century. However the additional records that there are available are dealt with. These are not entirely relevant for most people, as being for the most part based on property; they contain no reference to the "men of no property".

For those who are not in Ireland many of the records referred to can be obtained by contacting a repository directly or by going to a local genealogical repository or by accessing the Internet. The best genealogical repositories that I am aware of are the Family History Centres of the LDS Family History Library. Many genealogical societies have their own libraries; a person should seek to make contact with such societies. A local public library should be a guide to what is available and may have some records available.

The Internet is what I feel genealogy has been waiting for. The potential lies in the amount of data, which will become available and the opportunity to share information and exchange views with others. Material is being added to the Internet every day and the time will come when most genealogical research will be conducted through it. The book may be used in conjunction with my websites, in all cases websites are given where available, and such are linked to from my own site.

In December 2000 I set up a website *www.IrishAncestors.net*, this is my principal site for genealogical research. In addition I have now established other sites: *www.IrishSurnames.net* for general information on Irish surnames; *www.IrishSurnames.info* for information upon specific surnames in Ireland; and *www.QuinnSurname.com* dealing specifically with my own surname. The information upon surnames is based upon my book *Surnames in Ireland*.

Seán ó Cuinn / Seán E. Quinn
seanquinn@donegal.net
11th June 2002

Contents

Chapter 1

Introduction to genealogical research

The purpose of this book is to help you to trace your Irish ancestry by giving an account of what is involved in Irish genealogical research. This book seeks to answers many of the basic questions that might be asked by those interested in their Irish ancestry.

This book assumes that you have no knowledge at all of genealogical research. It will take you step by step through the process of drawing up your family tree. You must always keep at the back of your mind that in genealogy a person must go from the known to the unknown.

First steps
The first step is to ask yourself some questions about the ancestor or ancestors that you are interested in, such as the following:

Date of birth
Place of birth
Names of parents
Religion
Trade, profession, occupation or employment
To whom married
Where married
Names of children
Any other information

Which branch of your family are you going to trace? The further back you go, the more branches your family tree will have, and these branches will divide into more branches and so on. It is simpler to start on your paternal line, since you have to follow only one surname.

If you come to a stop with your paternal line, leave it for a while, and follow another line. There will always be plenty of branches to follow. In your great grandfather's generation, there are eight different surnames and all may be of interest to you. "Ancestor" is defined as a person from whom one's father or mother is descended and tracing your ancestors should not be confined to the paternal line only.

Preliminary research
The next step is to talk to your family and make a note of what they have to say. You should then gather up all the information possible from documents, such as certificates of birth, marriage and death from graveyard inscriptions from memoriam cards and whatever else can be got

1

hold of. With the information now obtained, you are in a position to talk to an elderly relative.

A grandparent would be the best relative from whom to obtain information. If a grandparent is not available, any grandaunt, granduncle or elderly relation possessing a sharp mind can do as well.

The opportunity to talk to an elderly relative should be taken immediately, before it is to late. It should prove a worthwhile exercise as old people like to talk about the past and do not always find someone who is prepared to listen. Always make a note of anything that you are told or use a tape recorder. Afterwards the information obtained should be written down.

When sitting down with an elderly person to inquire into your family background, you should bear the following in mind:
1. Give yourself plenty of time.
2. Be careful of hearsay (something heard from somebody else and not known directly). The story is told that during the Great War (1914-1918) a message went down the trenches by word of mouth "Send up reinforcements, we are going to advance", it was received as "Send up three and four pence (three shillings and four pence), we are going to a dance".
3. Tell the person to whom you are speaking little, so as to avoid it being repeated to you later and you treating it as confirmation.
4. Be patient.
5. Use your discretion when it comes to illegitimate births.

Mode of questioning
Be systematic in your questioning:
> At what age did he/she die?
> Was he/she the eldest in that family?
> What was the age difference between him/her and the eldest in the family? (This will give you an indication of a date of marriage)
> Was there any age difference between the father and mother?
> What ages were they when they got married?
> Where did the father and mother come in their own families?

The following should also be borne in mind at this stage and later when going through the registers of births: Within a year of marriage, a child was usually born and every one or two years thereafter during the mother's fertile years.

Children were nearly always called after someone and it was the custom to call the first boy after his paternal grandfather, the second boy after his maternal grandfather, a third boy might have been called after his own father, an uncle, or grand-uncle on either side of the family. The first and second girl may have been called after the grandmothers and a third girl, after her own mother or an aunt. It is only in the present generation that this practice has begun to wane.

Verify in the records

Do not treat all that you are told by your family and by relations as fact, verification must be sought in the records. For example: The family owned certain property, but were swindled out of it; the swindler or his descendants will often be named (but the story may not be true); members of the family went to America and were never heard of again (they may never have existed in the first place); An ancestor held high rank in the Army or Police (people are always promoted in the telling).

Geographical origin of ancestor

It can be difficult for those abroad to identify which part of Ireland an ancestor may have come from. It may have been passed down through the generations that an ancestor would have come from a seaport, such as Belfast, Cork, Derry, Dublin etc.. It becomes more difficult when an Irish ancestor may have sailed from Liverpool, England. There can be no doubt that a person would have traveled to these ports in order to sail from Ireland.

Where there is a lack of other evidence available to identify a place of origin, the surname may be the key. Irish surnames are to be found in particular localities, and where both surnames of a married couple are known identification is easier. In addition some personal names are particular to certain localities. Chapter 14 on the county distribution of surnames should prove a useful tool in this quest.

How far back can you go?

After searching through the records referred to in the following chapters, the majority of Irish people are most unlikely to be able to trace their ancestors back further than the late eighteenth century. This is because the earlier records are based on the ownership of property and, as practically the entire Irish population was dispossessed in the seventeenth century, any records of their existence are scarce.

Administrative divisions

There are many administrative divisions that one will come across as one goes through the records. What follows is a brief summary of them.

Province: They are Ulster; Munster; Leinster and Connaught. In Gaelic the term is *Cuige* meaning a fifth, their originally being a province of North Leinster/Meath.

County: Ireland was shired into counties beginning in the twelfth century and the process was completed in the seventeenth century with the Plantation of Ulster (1609). The county boundaries correspond with the principal Gaelic lordships of that period.

Diocese: The dioceses are administrative divisions of the Churches, they date from the twelfth century. The boundaries of the diocese represent ancient Gaelic territories of that time. A search of the parish registers will require the identification of an area within its dioceses.

Barony: The tuath was a basic division of Gaelic Ireland and it corresponded to the territory of a sept. The Barony was largely based upon this division. There are a number of baronies in each county. The Barony was used for many of the surveys of the 17th century. The establishment of the County Councils in 1898 saw the barony lose its significance.

Poor Law Union: The Poor Relief (Ireland) Act 1838, established the poor law unions as districts within which the inhabitants were responsible for the poor of the area. The poor law Unions embraced a number of townlands within a radius of ten miles or so, with a large market town as a centre. The boundaries of the Unions bore no relationship to those of the Counties.

Parish: The parish was an area over which a local church had jurisdiction. The civil administration made use of this division, hence civil parish. Many of the genealogical records to be consulted, will require a knowledge of the parochial boundary. The Parish is made up of townlands.

Townland: The townland is the smallest administrative division of land in Ireland. There are approximately 64,000 townlands. The present townlands date from 1837, when they were based upon the ancient ballyboe. The ballyboe was an area of land that would feed one cow. This explains why the larger townlands are found in the areas of poorest land.

Chapter 2

Census Returns

A census of Ireland was taken in 1813 and every 10 years from 1821. However very little has survived of the returns prior to 1901. There are some returns from the census of 1821, 1831, 1841 and 1851, covering part of the counties of Antrim, Cavan, Cork, Derry, Fermanagh, Galway, Meath Offaly and Waterford. There are no enumerators returns from the census of 1861, 1871, 1881, or 1891, these were destroyed by Government order.

The Census Returns may be inspected at the National Archives and in the Public Records Office. They have been microfilmed by the LDS (Mormons) and would be available through branch libraries. Largy Books of Alberta, Canada has published on microfiche an index of the 1901 Census for some counties. Information for some localities is now online and may be accessed via *www.IrishAncestors.net*. Returns for 1926 and subsequent censuses are not open to the public.

The appendices to the 55th Report (IV) and the 56th Report (VI) of the Deputy Keeper of Public Records, detail what is available.

Census 28th May 1821
These returns list; names, ages, occupations, and relationships.
What has survived and is available for consultation in the National Archives is:
County Cavan: Parishes of Annageliffe, Ballymacue, Castlerahan, Castleterra, Crosserlough, Denn, Drumlummon, Drung and Larah, Kilbride, Kilmore, Kinawley, Lavey, Lurgan and Munsterconaght, Mullagh.
County Fermanagh: Parishes of Derryvullen and Aghalurcher.
County Galway: Baronies of Arran and Athenry. Copies of returns for various families (58th Report, p. 33).
County Louth: A number of extracts for families principally relating to Drogheda (55th Report, p. 110).
County Meath: Baronies of Upper and Lower Navan.
County Offaly: Barony of Ballybritt (including Birr).
County Tipperary: Clonmel heads of households (58th R., p. 44).
Counties Cork, Mayo, Roscommon and Sligo: Copies of returns for various families (58th Report, p. 33).

Census 1831
These returns list; names, ages, religion, occupations and relationships.

What has survived and is available for consultation in the National Archives is:

County Derry: Parishes of Agivey, Macosquin, Ballyaghran, Killowen, Aghanloo, Tamlaght, Finlagan, Templemore, Arboe, Termoneeny, Banagher, Glendermot.

Census 6th June 1841

These returns list; names, ages, date of marriage, occupations, relationships and whether each person can read or write.

What has survived and is available for consultation in the National Archives is:

County Cavan: Parish of Killeshandra.

County Fermanagh: Parish of Currin.

County Waterford: Parish of Lismore.

Counties Cavan and Monaghan: Miscellaneous extracts for various names (58th Report, p. 18).

Census 30th March 1851

These returns list; names, ages, date of marriage, religion, occupations, relationships and whether each person can read or write.

What has survived and is available for consultation in the National Archives is:

County Antrim: Parishes of Tickmacrevan, Carncastle, Grange of Killyglen, Kilwaugher, Larne, Craigs (Ahoghill), Ballymoney, Donaghy, Rasharkin, Killead, Aghagallon, Aghalee, Ballinderry.

County Cavan: Miscellaneous extracts for various names (58th Report, p. 18).

County Fermanagh: Parish of Drumheeran.

Counties Cavan and Monaghan: Miscellaneous extracts for various names (58th Report, p. 18).

Census Search Forms

The census search forms or "Green Forms" were completed by the Public Records Office from information supplied by applicants for the Old Age Pension (which was introduced in 1908) seeking evidence of their age. A person had to be 70 years of age for the pension. The forms were drawn up between 1910 and 1922 and were an internal office record of searches made in the census of 1841 and 1851. An applicant provided information by letter and where there were sufficient details a search was carried out. A certified copy of the return was then issued. The documents are arranged by County, Barony, Parish, Townland/Street and surname of family searched. The information contained in these forms is varied.

Census 31st March 1901

The complete returns for this census and the census of 1911 have survived for all Ireland and are available for consultation in the National Archives in Dublin. Those for the six counties are in the Public Records Office, Belfast and in other repositories referred to later on microfilm.

If you wish to see the returns for a particular townland or street, you must first establish:

(a) the District Electoral Division number in the Townland Index for 1901 and the supplement for 1911, or the street indexes for Belfast, Cork, Dublin, Kingstown (Dun Laoghaire) and Limerick; and

(b) the townland or street number in the list of census returns for the year and county in question.

The original forms, which you will be able to consult, are arranged by townlands or, in urban areas by streets and consist of:

Form A filled in by the head of each household (more than likely your great grandparent); and

Forms N, B1, and B2 filled in by the official taking the Census usually a member of the Royal Irish Constabulary summarizing the returns for that townland or street.

Form A (1901 census) contained the following information:

Christian name and Surname of the head of the family, his wife, children and other relatives and also the names of visitors, boarders and servants who slept in the house on the night of Sunday 31st March 1901;

Relationship of each person to the head of household i.e. mother, wife, daughter, son, uncle, cousin;

Religious profession of each person;

Whether each person can "read and write", "can read only" or "cannot read";

Age in years of each person and in months for infant under one year;

Sex of each person;

The rank, profession or occupation of each person i.e. Farmer, Farm servant, Seamstress, Scholar;

Whether each person is "married"; "widower"; "widow"; or "not married";

Where each person was born e.g. Co. Donegal;

Irish language knowledge of each person i.e. "Irish", "Irish & English";

Whether any person is "deaf and dumb", "dumb only", blind", "imbecile", "idiot", or "lunatic".

Census 2nd April 1911

Form A for the 1911 Census contains all of the above for the night of Sunday the 2nd April 1911 with the following additional information in respect of married women:

Number of completed years of marriage;

Number of children born alive;

Number of children still living;

These questions were added in order to gather information on the fertility of marriages. The information as to the number of completed years of marriage can direct one towards a marriage certificate; unfortunately it is not filled in some returns.

These records are an invaluable source for tracing your family tree and there should be no difficulty in getting access very quickly to the records for the townlands and parishes in which you are interested.

It can be seen that there is quite an amount of information and one can be reasonably confident of the accuracy of the information that is provided. A word of warning however, because of the introduction of the old age pension in 1908, older people put on more than the natural ten years between 1901 and 1911 the more common increase to be found is from fifteen to twenty years within that ten years period.

It should now be possible to accurately estimate, dates of birth and marriage. This will assist in searching the civil registers of births, marriages and deaths and the parish registers. These are dealt with in the next two Chapters.

The Civil Survey
1654-1656
Counties of Donegal, London-Derry and Tyrone

VOLUME III
as prepared for publication by
Robert C. Simington
of the Quit Rent Office, Dublin.
Published by the Stationary Office on behalf of
the Irish Manuscripts Commission in 1937

$75 *Post Free*

From Seán E. Quinn, 57 Glenoughty Close, Letterkenny, Co. Donegal, Ireland.

Chapter 3

Civil Registration

The Marriages (Ireland) Act 1844 provided for the registration of marriages (except those celebrated by the Roman Catholic Clergy) with effect from 1st April 1845. The Registration of Births and Deaths (Ireland) Act 1863 provided for the registration of births and deaths with effect from 1st January 1864. Civil registration of births and deaths began later in Ireland than elsewhere. In England and Wales registration began on 1st. July 1837 and in Scotland on 1st. January 1855. Many Irish were born, married and died in Britain so such registrations should not be ignored.

Ireland was divided into Registrar's Districts, each under the charge of a local registrar, to whose office the registrations were made. There were about 800 Registrar's Districts and these were grouped into 140 Unions. The Registrar of the Union was responsible for collecting the registrations made by his district registrars, and he returned them to the Registrar General in Dublin. The Registrar-General's office then compiled composite indices for the whole country.

The indexes
There are volumes which list alphabetically all the entries contained in the registers. The indexes of birth, marriage and death are separate and are in chronological order.

In the volumes, each year is divided into quarters: March, June, September and December.
The quarters are divided as follows:
March quarter entries January, February, March
June quarter entries April, May, June
September quarter entries July, August, September
December quarter entries October, November, December.
Each quarter is divided alphabetically.
The indexes will list the name of the person alphabetically (Surname and Christian name), the Union where registered, the volume and page in the register as follows: Surname, District, Volume and Page.
The Union is the only guide to the address; remember that the Unions crossed county boundaries. The author has found mistakes in the indexes, so one should be aware of that.

You should remember that registration of an event may not necessarily take place on the same date as the event. Registration could have taken place some time later, so that if you are looking for and event which

9

occurred in September it may be recorded in either the September or the December quarter.

Remember while you are searching these records, that it is best to start with someone you know. Start one year before the birth. In genealogical research you must (as stated earlier) always go from the known to the unknown. If you are unsure of Christian names, remember the tradition as to the naming of children (see Chapter 1).

Birth certificate
The information contained at each entry for which a certificate can be issued is as follows:

>District
>Reference number
>Date of birth
>Place of birth
>Name of child
>Sex of child
>Name & dwelling place of father
>Name & maiden name of mother
>Rank or profession of father
>Informant (usually a parent)

A child may have been registered in the maiden name of the mother. The index will only provide the name of the child. This can present difficulties with a numerous surname. It would be of great assistance to genealogists if the index could also show the name of the parents. At the present time indexes are being prepared showing the maiden name of the mother. Seeking a child with an unusual surname is easiest. It should not be assumed that all births were registered. In the early years of registration, many births were not recorded.

A birth certificate will provide you with the exact date of birth, the names of both parents and an address. If you do not already have such information they are worthwhile.

Marriage certificate
The information contained at each entry for which a certificate can be issued is as follows:

>District (usually the home place of wife)
>Reference number
>Date of marriage
>Place of marriage
>Name & Surname of both parties

Age of each party (Unfortunately it often gives "of full age" that is over 21 rather than the actual age)
Condition of each i.e. Bachelor/Widower, Spinster/Widow
Rank or profession of each
Residence of each at time of marriage
Fathers of each: Name & Surname; Rank or Profession

It often happened that a widow and widower would marry each other. If a widow remarries the name on the marriage certificate is not the maiden name, but her previous married surname.

Marriage certificates are most useful. They give most information and bring one back a further generation, because they give the names of both fathers. There are few errors in the Index of Marriages and given that the two parties are listed, there is verification in the index itself. With marriages you can cross check the index by looking for the marriage partner.

One should not waste time searching for a marriage of unknown date. It is possible to get a good idea of the date from the censuses of 1901 and 1911 (this will actually state how long the marriage has lasted). There should be no difficulty tracing a marriage, if the names of both parties are known. If you have no information on the wife, you should firstly seek a birth certificate of a child of the marriage. This will give the mother's maiden name.

Death certificate
The information contained at each entry for which a certificate can be issued is as follows:

District
Reference number
Place of death
Date of death
Surname
Christian name & Sex of deceased
Marital status
Age
Rank or Profession
Cause of death
Informant (usually a relative)

It can be seen that the death certificate offers the least information. In addition it cannot be assumed that the age at death is correct. A death certificate will verify a date and place of death, if you are seeking such information. If you do not know a date of death, it might not be worth the time spent finding it out.

Where to find the records

The principal repositories of the civil records, their location (in Dublin and Belfast) and fees are considered in Chapter 11. In Belfast the Public Records Office (see Chapter 10) has copies of the printed indexes of births, registered in the whole of Ireland for the period 1864 - 1922. In addition the Public Records Office also has the original Register of births and Register of deaths for the Six Counties.

The Family History Library in (see Chapter 12) has microfilm copies of all the indexes to 1958 (to 1959 in the case of the Six Counties); of marriage and death registers to 1871; of birth registers to 1881 and from 1900 to 1913; birth registers 1930 to 1955 (for Twenty-Six Counties); birth, marriage and death registers from 1922 to 1959 (Six Counties). A General Index of Births registered in Ireland for 1864, 1865 and 1866 was published in 1873. This is available in the National Library of Ireland. Throughout Ireland there are local registration offices, many of which will allow you to search through the actual registers. From 2003 these records might be available to search via the Internet.

Mode of inquiry

The recommended mode of inquiry to be followed when searching through the civil and parish registers is best considered in two stages:
Stage one

On the basis of information already obtained, estimate the date of birth of eldest child of a family, and then find the birth (baptism) certificate of this child which will verify the name of both parents.
Stage two

A birth (or baptism) certificate of the eldest child generally indicates a marriage during the previous year. An estimate of the year of marriage can then be made and a marriage certificate obtained. This will indicate (in the case of the civil registers) the dates of birth of the parents and give the names of the grandfathers (grandmothers are not noted).

The birth certificate of the husband and wife (or their eldest brother or sister) can then be sought and the process begun again

This can be continued back in time until one is faced with the problem that the civil records only began in 1864 (or 1845 as the case may be). However with the information obtained from the Baptism, Burial and Marriage entries you may now have got back a further generation.

The next step is to move on to the parish registers of the churches, which are dealt with in the following Chapter

Chapter 4

Parish Registers of the Churches

The parish registers of the various religious denominations take on an added importance, for the period prior to 1864 or 1845 (as the case may be) because civil registration began so late in Ireland. The parish registers in Ireland are circumscribed by the restrictions imposed on the Catholic Church in penal times.

The repositories where the parish registers may be consulted are considered in later Chapters, though brief mention is made of them in this Chapter. The repositories have on open access: details of the parish registers that they have available for consultation.

Irish and Scotch-Irish Ancestral Research by Falley lists which parish registers are available for consultation and their starting date. *A Guide to Irish Parish Registers* edited by Mitchell may also be consulted for this information. The Irish Family History Society has a publication entitled *Directory of Parish Registers Indexed in Ireland*, which should prove useful.

There is on microfiche and available for consultation in the LDS Family History Centres (see Chapter 13) the International Genealogical Index (IGI). It is compiled predominantly from parish registers and is a convenient way to prepare for searching parish registers. This can also be searched at *www.familysearch.com*. In addition many parish registers have been computerized at a local level. It follows that where a person has exhausted the central repositories enquiries should then be made at a local level.

Catholic Church
The penal laws effectively outlawed the Catholic Church and in those circumstances it was not feasible for records to be kept. The Catholic Emancipation Act 1829 put an end to the penal laws. The Catholic Church, nevertheless required the clergy to keep records of baptisms, marriages and burials. However it was not until very late, that this was carried out in rural areas. The earliest parish registers date from the beginning of the nineteenth century and many particularly in the west, only begin after the records of civil registration.

The information available in the Catholic parish registers varies, as follows
    <u>Baptisms</u>:
                Name of child
                Whether child was illegitimate

Date of Baptism
Names of parents
Residence of parents
God-parents (who were often relations)

Marriages:

Date of marriage
Names of parties
Residence of parties
Witnesses (sometimes)
Fathers' names (sometimes)
Fathers' residence (sometimes)

Going through these registers is a tedious job as many of the records are faded and incomplete. Latin is often used rather than English (or Irish). A person should not forget to seek out the Burial Registers of the Church of Ireland referred to below.

The parishes of the Catholic Church did not always coincide with the civil parishes and this should be remembered when one is preparing for a search through Catholic parish registers. *The Townlands Index to Ireland,* will show the civil parish in which a townland is situated. *The Topographical Dictionary of Ireland* by Samuel Lewis (1837) should then be consulted. The Index of Surnames to the Primary Valuation and the Tithe Books prepared by the National Library of Ireland lists the civil parishes and the equivalent Catholic parishes and this is available in the principal repositories.

Most of the parish registers prior to 1880 are available on microfilm in the National Library of Ireland. The microfilms may be freely consulted except in the case of parishes of the following dioceses: Ardagh and Clonmacnoise, Cloyne, Down and Connor, Galway, Kerry and Limerick. In the case of theses dioceses a letter of authorisation from the Parish Priest concerned must be produced before those microfilms may be consulted. The *Catholic Directory* (issued annually) lists the Catholic clergy and contains the names of the Parish Priests. This is useful if a person is seeking access to the closed registers and if one wishes to arrange access to registers locally.

It will not always be necessary to go to the National Library of Ireland to consult these registers. A person may go along to the parish church of the ancestor concerned the registrar will without doubt be easier to read than the microfilms. It is important to be aware that there are Catholic parish registers in the custody of the local clergy, the existence of which are not always recorded elsewhere.

The Public Records Office in Belfast has available a list of Catholic parish registers in local custody in the Six Counties.

Church of Ireland

It was required in 1634 that "in every parish church or chapel within this realm shall be provided one parchment book at the charge of the parish wherein shall be written the day and the year of every christening and burial". Consequently a number of Church of Ireland parish registers date from the seventeenth century.

The Irish Church Act 1869 led to the disestablishment of the Church of Ireland with effect from the 1st January 1871. The Parochial Records Acts 1875 and 1876 stipulated that the records of the Church of Ireland constituted public records and as such were to be handed over to the Public Records Office. However, where an adequate place of storage was available locally they were allowed to remain in local custody.

In 1922 the pre-1871 records of 1006 parishes were destroyed by fire in the Public Records Office. The records of 637 parishes, which were in the custody of the local clergy survived. The Appendix to the 14th Report of the Assistant Deputy Keeper, 1881-83 has a "Table of Parochial Records in the Public Records Office" and the appendix to the 28th Report of the Deputy Keeper has a list of records in local custody. The appendices to the 56th, 57th. and 58th. Reports of the Deputy Keeper have details of the surviving parish registers and of transcripts of destroyed parish registers.

An up to date list of the surviving registers specifying their whereabouts, is available in the reading room of the National Archives (see Chapter 9). The Public Records Office in Belfast (see Chapter 10) has much material.

Many Church of Ireland parish registers relating to Dublin were published prior to 1922. They cover the period from 1619 to 1825. In pre-famine Ireland, it was common for all Christian denominations to be buried in the same graveyard, thus the burial registers of the Church of Ireland will list members of other denominations.

The parishes of the Church of Ireland generally coincide with the civil parishes and there should be no difficulties as to location.

The information available in these registers varies, as follows:

Baptisms:
- Name of child
- Date of Baptism
- Names of Father
- Name of Mother (sometimes)
- Occupation of Father
- Residence of parents

Marriages:
- Date of marriage
- Names of parties
- Residence of parties

Burial entries:
> Name
> Date of death
> Age (sometimes)
> Occupation (sometimes)
> Relationships (sometimes)

The Representative Church Body Library in Dublin (see Chapter 13) holds the Church of Ireland archives and over the years has done a great deal of work to repair the loss of parish registers in 1922. Most registers do not have indexes and there is no single index to all their contents. It is better to have a name, a date, and a place name. However some registers have been indexed on a county basis.

Given the difficulties of access in relation to civil records and that these registers should be intact from 1871, a visit should be made to the parish you are interested in and permission sought to examine the actual registers. The *Irish Church Directory* (issued annually) gives the names and addresses of all Church of Ireland clergy. The clergy are required to make the registers available. However they are required to supervise searches and a fee is payable.

Presbyterian Church
The Presbyterian Church is the third of the main Christian denominations in Ireland. The ancestors of most Presbyterians in Ireland arrived during the Plantation of Ulster from the lowlands of Scotland. Subsequently there was settlement in Antrim and Down as well as the six plantation counties of Armagh, Cavan, Derry, Donegal, Fermanagh and Tyrone.

The Presbyterian Historical Society Library (see Chapter 13) in Belfast has deposited in its vaults the oldest parish registers dating from the seventeenth century. Many of these are now on microfilm; in the Public Records Office Belfast and in the library itself. Most congregations have retained their registers in local custody. The library has an index covering the Presbyterian Church registers of the 367 congregations in Ireland. The earliest records of some congregations have been published.

Presbyterian births and marriages will also be found in the parish registers of the Church of Ireland. In order to gain access to the registers in local custody, contact should be made with the Minister of the congregation.

The Primary Valuation of Tenements and Tithe Applotment Composition Books will now add to the information already obtained and they are considered in the next two Chapters.

Chapter 5

The Primary Valuation of Tenements

The Primary Valuation was a survey made under the Act of 1838 to determine the amount of tax each able person should pay towards support of the poor and destitute within his poor law union. The value of all lands and buildings was calculated to determine the annual rental of each property. The tax was fixed at about 6d in the £ and the Act required that the occupiers, tenants, and the immediate lessors were liable for the tax.
It took sixteen years to complete the survey from 1848 to 1864. The work was carried out under the direction of Richard Griffith and for this reason is commonly known as "Griffith's Valuation".

Information contained
The Primary Valuation of Rateable Property In Ireland was published, on a baronial basis, after its completion by the Government. Each poor law union is divided into electoral divisions, civil parishes and townlands. Included are the names of occupiers of land and buildings and of the persons from whom these were leased, the amount of property held, and the value assigned to it. The information in respect of each townland, listed in the parish to which it belongs, is as follows:

> Number and Letters of Reference to Map -
> Names -
>> Occupier
>> Immediate lessor
> Description of Tenement - (House office or land)
>> Area: acres, roods, perches
> Rateable Annual Valuation -
>> Land
>> Buildings
> Total Annual Valuation of Rateable Property -

The map reference number is to the location of the tenement on the six inch to one mile Ordnance Survey maps of the 1830's.

The Primary Valuation therefore provides a census of all who held property in the year or years that the survey was made. It is of great genealogical value and a good census substitute.

The majority of the occupiers of the townlands in "Griffith's Valuation" were the ancestors of families that are living in these same townlands at the present time. It is only in recent years that those who stayed in Ireland married outside their own locality. On finding an ancestor in the Primary

Valuation, it is likely that a number of ancestors will be found in the adjoining townlands of the same parish as well.

The name of the father of a person born during the 1850's should be found in the Primary Valuation. The person so found would most likely have been born during the period of 1800 to 1830. The death certificate of a person listed in the Primary Valuation should be found in the civil registers.

The Primary Valuation is itself a valuable guide for the use of other genealogical sources. The name of the "Immediate Lessors" would be of assistance in seeking out Estate Records, which may have additional information on an ancestor. The same information could be a lead to sources in the Registry of Deeds (see Chapter 12).

Index
The National Library of Ireland has prepared an index to the surnames in the Primary Valuation (the same index covers the Tithe Books). Each County of Ireland has an index book. The number of occupiers having a particular surname is listed by barony and also by parish. It is possible to search through the townlands to find occupiers' bearing the surname that one is interested in. The indexation of the actual names of persons in the Primary Valuation on a county basis has been undertaken in some instances. The Primary Valuation is available in the National Library of Ireland (on microfiche), in the National Archives, in the Public Records Office Belfast and in many other repositories. Most County Libraries have the valuation for their particular county. The Genealogical Publishing Company of Baltimore has published a CD Index.

Manuscript valuation books
The manuscript records of the valuation which include the returns of the valuators provide more information than has been published.
There are three types of books:
House books - Number, name and description, quality letter, length, breath, height, number of measures, rate per measure, amount.
Tenure books - content of farm, rent, tenure and year let, observations.
Field books - number of lot, description of lot, quantity, value per statute acre, amount of land £. s. d., amount of houses.
These are in the National Archives and are indexed by county.

Estate records
The Primary Valuation can give a lead to estate records that might refer to an ancestor. Estate records can be found in the National Library, the National Archives, and the Public Records Office in Belfast.

Chapter 6

Tithe Composition and Applotment Books

Tithes were payable by all, regardless of their religion to the established Church of Ireland prior to disestablishment. The Tithe Composition Acts provided, beginning in July 1823, for the payment of tithes to the clergy of each parish of the Church of Ireland in money rather than payment in kind as had been the position before. This new method of payment involved a valuation of the country parish by parish under the direction of parochial commissioners, one of whom was elected by the ratepayers and the other nominated by the Bishop of the Diocese.

The books were complied between 1823 and 1838 as a survey of the tithable land in each parish. The Catholic Emancipation Act 1928 had not been enacted when the tithe valuation had become law and Catholic parish registers are not generally available for this period. It has been stated that "It was the first complete register of the people in relation to the working and tenancy of the land, and its worth is heightened by the fact that it is a duly certified recording of the occupation and usage of the land for the two decades immediately proceeding the upheaval wrought by the Famine of 1847". After the Famine, people dispersed themselves throughout the townlands rather than living in clusters and many dispersed themselves further by emigrating.

Between the years 1823 and 1830, 1,353 parishes out of 2,450 parishes in Ireland had been accessed. The Tithe Books do not cover towns or cities. Tithe Books are not available for all parishes, in some cases this is because the parish did not exist at the time, or was united with another parish at the time of the tithe survey and the area surveyed as part of another parish.

The land divisions contained in the Tithe Books are not the same as the present divisions, which exist from the Ordnance Survey of 1837. Because of this the Tithe Books are a record of the sub-divisions that comprised each parish in quarterlands, ploughlands and townlands and the names of such sub-divisions, as they were known at that time.

Information contained
The information contained varies but can include:
                    Name of the occupier
                    Name of townland
                    Acreage
                    Classification of land - into four classes
                    The amount of tithe

Areas not subject to tithe
Landlords' names

An ancestor found in the Tithe Books would most probably have been born during the period 1780 to 1800. It is possible that a person that you come across could be the father of a person listed in the Primary Valuation, given the lapse of a generation.

Where available
The Tithe Books, numbering two and a half thousand manuscript volumes, were transferred from the custody of the Commissioners of Church Temporalities to the Land Commission and from there to the Public Records Offices.

The Tithe Books will now be found in the National Archives (for the Twenty Six Counties) and in the Public Records Office Belfast (for the Six Counties). The National Library of Ireland has microfilm copies of the Tithe Books for the Six Counties. The Public Records Office in Belfast has a card index of names contained in the Tithe Books covering Ulster. In addition to the index of surnames, which also cover the Primary Valuation, there is an index by parish and county. In the index of surnames the letter "T" distinguishes a surname that is contained in the Tithe Books. The indexation of actual names in the Tithe Books on a county basis has been undertaken in the past as part of local youth employment schemes.

The Genealogical Publishing Company of Baltimore has published a CD Index to the Tithe Books for the Six Counties.

Chapter 7

Additional Genealogical Sources

The following additional sources are listed in chronological order.

Inquisitions Post Mortem
An Act of Parliament abolished the holding of land by feudal tenure during the reign of Charles II. The Inquisition Post Mortem give the descent of families, the possession and transfer of land from the time of Elizabeth I to that of Charles II. They give the name of the deceased, date of death, name and age of their heir, together with particulars as to the property.
The Inquisitions for Leinster and Ulster were published in 1826. Those for Munster and Connaught are available in the National Archives and in the Royal Irish Academy. There is an index to all Inquisitions in the supplement to the 8th Report of the Record Commissioners (1819).

Calendar of Irish Patent Rolls of James 1
A Patent Roll was a grant of land to a person from the King, the Patent Rolls give the name of the grantee and sometimes the reason for the grant. The Calendar of Irish Patent Rolls of James I was edited by and published by the Irish Manuscripts Commission in 1966.

Ulster Plantation 1609
The Presbyterian Historical Society Library in Belfast has a list of Scottish Freeholders in the Ulster Plantation.

Muster Roll 1630
It was a condition, binding on the undertakers in the Plantation of Ulster that they should "have ready in their houses at all times, a convenient store of Arms, wherewith they may furnish a competent number of men for their defence".
A return of those available was drawn up by William Graham, in or around the year 1630. The original is in the British Library (Add. Ms 4770). It is available both, in the Presbyterian Historical Library and the Public Records Office in Belfast. The lists for Cavan, Donegal and Fermanagh, have been printed in local journals/histories.

Subsidy Roll 1634
Those who paid a grant in aid of the King are listed in the Subsidy Rolls. The Representative Church Body Library in Dublin has transcripts made by Tenison Groves of the Subsidy Roll of 1634, which is indexed (see below).

Muster Roll 1642

The Rising of 1641 resulted in another muster. The Public records Office in Belfast has a Muster Roll for County Down 1642, there is a copy in the Presbyterian Historical Society Library.

Calendar of Patent Rolls of Charles I

Calendar of Patent Rolls Ireland Charles I Vol. 1 edited by J. Morrin was published in Dublin in 1863.

List of Outlaws 1641-47

After the failure of the Rising of 1641, many of Irish landowners were outlawed. This resulted in two and a half million Irish acres being confiscated. The list consists of 2,200 names and the information given is: Names, Place of Residence, Title/Occupation, Date of Outlawry and Place of Outlawry. An abstract in English of the records for the periods 1641-71 are in the library of the Oireachtas. The National Library of Ireland has microfilm copies of it (see also below).

Civil Survey of Ireland 1654

This was carried out by order of the English Parliamentary Government, the war that had been waged in Ireland was to be paid for with Irish land. It lists the landlords of each townland and their predecessors in 1641. It has been published by the Irish Manuscripts Commission and the parts that are available are for the following counties: Tipperary, Limerick, Waterford, Kerry (part of), Dublin (except the baronies of Newcastle and Uppercross), Kildare (except the barony of Ophaley), Meath, Wexford (except Forth), Donegal Derry and Tyrone (copies of this volume are available from myself). There is an article by J.G. Simms in Irish Historical Studies (1954-5) on the Civil Survey.

The Civil Survey
1654-1656
Counties of Donegal, London-Derry and Tyrone
VOLUME III
as prepared for publication by
Robert C. Simington
of the Quit Rent Office, Dublin.
Published by the Stationary Office on behalf of
the Irish Manuscripts Commission in 1937

$75 *Post Free*

Down Survey 1654

Sir William Petty carried this out. On 11th December 1654 he entered into agreement with the Commonwealth Government to " survey and admeassure,...all the forfeited lands, both profitable and unprofitable, within the baronies of the ten halfe counties appointed by ... for satisfaction of the arrears of the officers and soldiers in Ireland,.."It is a record of the ownership of land after the Cromwellian confiscations and the information was portrayed on parish and barony maps.

What survives of the Down Survey fall into three categories

(a) Copies of parish maps made in 1787 by the Hon R. Rochfort, Surveyor General which now form the Reeves collection in the National Library of Ireland,

(b) A series of Barony maps known as Hibernia Regnum compiled from the parish maps and representing the survey as a whole in diminutive form, this is in the Bibliotheque Nationale, Paris.

(c) The Quit Rent Office maps and tracings, now in the National Archives.

The National Library has the survey books for County Tipperary (M.95).

Census of Ireland 1659

This was compiled by Sir William Petty. *A Census of Ireland (c. 1659)* has been edited by Seamus Pender and published, with supplementary material on the Poll Money Ordinance (1660-1661), by the Irish Manuscripts Commission (1959). Now re-published.

The format was as follows: Parishes, Townlands Numbers of People Tituladoes Names Eng. (Scotts) Irish. It gives the names of those who held title to the land and the total number of persons (English and Irish) resident in each townland, it also lists the principal Irish names in each barony and their number. According to Pender the term "Titulado" is best explained as referring to the principal person or persons of standing in any particular locality; such a person could have been of either sex, a nobleman, baronet, gentleman, esquire, military officer, or adventurer. The classification under the heading English, Scots, or Irish is not completely accurate.

The census is arranged in counties, baronies, parishes and townlands and in cities parishes and streets. This includes details of population for the counties of: Ulster - Antrim, Armagh, Derry, Donegal, Down, Fermanagh, Monaghan, Munster - Clare, Cork and Cork city, Kerry, Limerick and Limerick city, Tipperary, Waterford and Waterford city, Leinster - Carlow, Dublin, and Dublin City, Kildare, Kilkenny, Laois, Longford, Louth, Meath Offaly, Westmeath, Wexford, Connaught - Leitrim, Roscommon, and Sligo. The volumes for Cork county and Meath are not complete.

Hearth Money Rolls 1665

The Hearth Money Act 1662 provided that there was to be a tax of two shillings on each hearth (chimney). The rolls consist of the names of householder who paid the hearth tax, it is arranged on a county, parish and townland basis.

The National Archives has copies of and extracts from the rolls for various place in Counties Armagh, Dublin, Fermanagh and Tyrone (M. 2468-74). There are also copies of the rolls available in the Public Records Office, Belfast, the National Library of Ireland (Ms 9583) and also in the Office of the Chief Herald (Ms 538). The Presbyterian Historical Society Library in Belfast has a transcript copy of the roll for County Antrim. The Representative Church Body Library in Dublin has copies of the returns indexed under Dioceses and Parishes.

They have been published for some counties in local journals.

Subsidy Roll 1669

The Irish Parliament during the 1660's, as a contribution towards the solution of the financial problems of Charles II, especially for the maintenance of the army in Ireland voted for a series of subsidies. All who owned goods worth at least £3 were taxed at the rate of 2s 8d in the pound. Assessment in each county was in the hands of Commissioners, who were to draw up lists of tax-payers and give them to the Sheriffs. A duplicate list together with the gross amounts to be paid was sent to the Exchequer. These duplicate lists and gross amounts are known as the Subsidy Rolls. The National Archives has some material from the Subsidy Rolls. The Subsidy Rolls for County Down 1663 are in the Public Records Office and in the Presbyterian Historical Society Library in Belfast.

King James II's Irish Army List 1689

Illustrations Historical and Genealogical of King James II's Irish Army List (1689) by John D'Alton, contains much information on those who served the Jacobite cause. The second edition was published in 1861.

Outlawry Lists 1691

In 1689 William III issued a declaration calling on those who supported James II to surrender, failing which their estates could be forfeited. As there was no response to this proceeding for high treason were to be instituted. After the Battle of the Boyne in 1690, proceedings were taken in the courts against those who had supported James II. Juries in a number of counties returned bills of indictment for high treason against more than two thousand individuals. Most of these persons were outlawed. After the war more than a thousand individuals, most of whom had joined the

French army were outlawed. The lists of outlawries are in Latin and record the names, addresses and status (or in some cases occupations). There are more than four thousand names. An abstract in English of the records for the periods 1641-71 and 1691-98 are in the library of the Oireachtas. The National Library of Ireland has microfilms of it.

Athlone Herald 1690
The Jacobite Court in exile had its own Herald, James Terry, who had to satisfy both the French and Spanish courts as to the pedigrees of those who sought advancement. *The Pedigrees & Papers of James Terry, Athlone Herald (1690-1725)* by C.E. Lart was published in 1938.

Books of Survey and Distributions c. 1700
The purpose of these books was to establish an official record of landed properties and their estates in order to levy the Quit Rent which was payable annually on lands granted under the Acts of Settlement and Explanation 1666-84. The restoration of the monarchy in England, with Charles II in 1660, meant a redistribution of land in Ireland to royalists who had been dispossessed.

The books list the ownership of land in each barony and parish prior to, and subsequent to, the forfeitures under the Parliamentary Government and William III. The names of the old proprietors, the lands forfeited, the extent profitable and unprofitable, and the areas distributed to the specified new owners are exhibited, column by column, in wide folios.

The proprietors of land circa 1700 are listed.

The manuscripts are available in the National Archives and the National Library of Ireland has on microfilm the records for every county except Meath. Duplicate copies of the Survey have survived, one of these sets, known as the Taylor Books is now in the Royal Irish Academy.
The Irish Manuscripts Commission has published the Books for Roscommon (1949), Mayo (1956), Galway (1962) and Clare (1967).

Convert Rolls 1704-1839
In order to avoid the legal disabilities imposed by the Penal Law, a number of Catholics renounced their religion for that of the established Church of Ireland. In the majority of cases this was not a sincere renunciation of the Catholic religion, as it was the only legal means whereby a Catholic could obtain basic civil rights. *The Convert Rolls*, cover the period from 1704 to 1839, in addition to the names, give the address and sometimes the names of parents. Edited by E. O'Brien they have been published by the Irish Manuscripts Commission (1981).

Voters Lists 1727-1793

Voters Lists contain the name and address of those entitled to vote, they do not record the way people voted. These lists cover either parishes or baronies. From 1727 to 1793 only Protestants with a freehold worth at least forty shillings per year had the vote, from 1793 to 1829 both Protestants and Catholics with forty shilling freeholds had the vote. In 1829 all forty shilling freeholders lost the vote. What is available is very scattered, the Public Records Office in Belfast has records for Ulster.

List of Protestant Householders 1740

This was compiled in 1740. It is a list of Protestant householders in parts of counties Antrim, Armagh, Derry, Donegal and Tyrone. It is arranged by county, barony and parish but not townland, only the names of householders are given. It is available in the Office of the Chief Herald (G. O. 539) and is typed and indexed. It is also available in the Representative Church Body Library but is not indexed.

Poll Books 1752

Poll Books are the books which recorded the votes cast at parliamentary elections, they contain the name (forty shilling freeholders) and address of the voter. The Office of the Chief Herald has the books for Armagh (1753) and Westmeath (1761). The Public Records Office Belfast has books for Antrim (1776), Armagh (1753) and Down (1852 and 1857).

Register of Freeholders 1758

Those who held a freehold worth less than forty shillings per annum and all Catholic freeholders prior to 1793 did not have a vote. The Office of the Chief Herald has lists of freeholders for counties: Laois (1758), Donegal (1761), Kilkenny, Meath and Tipperary (1775), Roscommon (1780) and Fermanagh (1788). The Public Records Office in Belfast has lists for the Ulster counties.

Militia Lists 1761

Is a list of men in a local militia aged between 16 and 60 years, able to bear arms. The Office of the Chief Herald has lists for the following counties: Cork. Derry, Donegal, Down, Dublin, Kerry, Limerick, Louth, Monaghan, Roscommon, Tipperary and Wicklow (M. 680). The Public Records Office in Belfast has lists for the Ulster counties (including Antrim, Armagh and Tyrone).

Roll of Electors 1761

The Roll of Electors (Protestants with forty shilling freeholds) is available for Donegal in the National Library of Ireland (Ms 787). There is also a freeholders list for Donegal in the Office of the Chief Herald.

Return of Householders 1766
In 1766, the Government instructed rectors of the Church of Ireland, to make a return of householders in their parishes, showing their religion (whether Protestant, Dissenter or Papist). It is also known as the "Religious Census 1766". The census lists the names of the head of the households, their religion and numbers of children. The counties for which transcripts are available include: Cork (part of), Derry, Limerick, Louth, Tipperary and Wicklow. The returns available vary in quality and some list only protestant households. What is available is in the National Archives, the Public Records Office Belfast, the Office of the Chief Herald (M. 536-7) and in the Representative Church Body Library. Local journals have published extracts of their own areas.

Freeholders entitled to vote 1770
The names of freeholders entitled to vote for counties Meath (1775 and 1781) and Longford (1790) are available in the National Library of Ireland. The National Archives has a list of electors (forty shilling freeholders) for County Longford (1790) (M.2486-8).

Oath of Allegiance 1775
Test book 1775-6 containing the names of Catholics taking the Oath of Allegiance under an Act passed in the Irish Parliament in 1775. This has been printed in the 59th Report of the Deputy Keeper of Public Records.

Catholic Qualification Rolls 1778/93
In 1778 the Irish Parliament passed an Act entitled "An Act for the relief of his Majesty's subjects in this Kingdom professing the Popish religion". The Act permitted Catholics to take leases for any term of years not exceeding nine hundred and ninety-nine or for any number of lives not exceeding five, provided that they had taken and subscribed the oath of allegiance passed in the Irish Parliament in 1774. The names of persons taking and subscribing the oath after 1778 were enrolled at the Rolls Office in Dublin. The index to these rolls survives, the information contained in the Index is usually; name, occupation, date and where oath was taken. The index is in the National Archives.

Flax Growers List 1796
The list was published by the Linen Board in 1796 and contains the names of flax growers who were eligible for assistance under a premium scheme.

In order to encourage the growing of flax, rather than it being imported, spinning wheels and utensils were to be given as a premium. It has been published and also available on CD-Rom.

State prisoners 1798
In his capacity as representative of the Crown, the Lord Lieutenant exercised the prerogative of mercy in Ireland. Many convicts submitted, or had submitted on their behalf, petitions for commutation or remission of their sentence. The petitions vary greatly in style and content but details to be found concern the crime, trial, sentence, place of origin and family circumstances of the convicts. The State Prisoners' Petitions petitions concern those arrested for involvement in the 1798 Rebellion, for which many were sentenced to transportation. The petitions are in the Sate Papers Office, have been microfilmed and indexed on computer. See also the consideration of transportation below.

Marriage Liscence Bonds
The Marriage Liscence Bonds which are considered in chapter 10 also cover the eighteenth century.

Grand Jurors and Books of Presentiments 1805
Grand Jury Presentments are the chief records of the county administration prior to 1898. These and Grand Warrants contain information about work ordered to be done by the Grand Jury. In addition there are Quarter Session and County Court records that could be consulted. Rate books, compiled for the collection of local government rates contain lists of householders and occupiers. The National Archives has records for the twenty-six counties. The Public Records Office in Belfast has such records for the six counties.

Tithe Applotment and Composition Books 1823 - 38
The Tithe Books are considered in chapter 6.

Transportation Records 1791-1853
Convicts transported to Australia in the first half of the 19th Century numbered approximately 40,000. The documents relating to such transportation were housed in the State Paper Office. Most valuable are the Petitions submitted by many of the convicts or their families seeking to reduce or change the sentence, these contain family and other details. These documents were microfilmed and are now online.

The first ship to sail directly from Ireland carrying convicts under sentence of transportation was the Queen, which arrived in Port Jackson on

26 September 1791. Transportation from Ireland to Australia came to an end in 1853. During this time some 30,000 men and 9,000 women were sent as convicts to Australia for a minimum period of seven years; many more followed their loved ones as free settlers. In 1868 sixty-three Fenians were transported from England.

Transportation Registers, 1836-1857 (TR) Microfilms 1-5
The transportation Registers contain over 20,000 names of men and women sentenced to transportation or death in the years 1836-57. The entries are divided by year, by county and by sex, and sometime give details of name of transport ship, commuted sentence or place of detention. The registers have been filmed and indexed in their entirety. Most of the convicts listed went to Australia, although some had their sentences commuted to terms of imprisonment to be served in Ireland, and others were transported to the penal establishments in Bermuda and Gibraltar. Of those sentenced to death, some had their sentences commuted to transportation, but others were hanged or were imprisoned.

Prisoners' Petitions and Cases, 1788-1836 (PPC) MF. 6-19
Many convicts submitted, or had submitted, petitions for commutation or remission of their sentence. The petitions vary greatly in style and content but details to be found concern the crime, trial, sentence, place of origin and family circumstances of the convicts.

State Prisoners' Petitions, 2798-99 (SPP) Microfilms 20-25
These are similar in content to the main series of petitions but concern those arrested for involvement in the 1798 Rebellion, for which many were sentenced to transportation.

Convict Reference Files, 1836-56; 1865-68 (CRF) MF. 101-4
These take over from the petitions series. In addition to petitions, they contain a variety of documents relating to individual convicts.

Free Settlers' Papers, 1828-52 (FS) Microfilms 101-104
Male convicts who had served a minimum of four years were entitled to request a free passage for dependents to join them in the colony. The papers comprise some lists with details of convicts who requested such a favour. There are also petitions from the convicts and from their wives, as well as a small number of personal letters written by convicts to their wives at home describing life in the colony.

Male Convict Register, 1842-47 Microfilm 104
This contains the names of all male convicts sentenced to transportation in the period 1842-7. In addition to the details contained in the transportation registers, some physical details are given.

Register of Convicts on Convict Ships, 1851-53
This single volume register contains the names of convicts (with date and county of trial) who embarked on ships sailing in that period to Van Diemen's Land (Tasmania) and Western Australia.

Computer Index
The names and other details of prisoners referred to in the five main series of records (TR, PPC, SPP, CRF, FS) have been entered in the computer database. In order to establish if there is any record of a particular individual, you should begin by searching the computer index. A successful search will produce one or more reference numbers, which will enable you to identify the relevant record or records in the microfilms.

Using the computer index
The search-by-surname option on the menu allows you to search for the name in two ways:
(1) By the surname with exact spelling and
(2) By surname with exact or similar spelling.
The details on each prisoner entered in the database should allow you to identify the individual you are seeking. These details include name, age, date and county of trial, crime and sentence. Where there is no date of trial available, the field 'date if document' will have an indication of the date of conviction. Finally the document reference number is given to allow you to consult the text of the original record on microfilm.

Emigration
It was only from January 1890 that Passenger list were kept of those departing from British and Irish ports, and these are at the Public Records Office in Kew. There was no clear record kept of the many millions that left the country prior to that date. Before the English began transporting the Irish as convicts to Australia, they had transported them to their colonies in North America. This began during the time of the Cromwellian Plantation, and in the year 1660 10,000 Irish children were shipped. The total so transported was estimated at between 60,000 and 100,000. The Irish were spread throughout the colonies, however the colony that attracted them most was Maryland Virginia. In the nineteenth century approximately 8 million people left Ireland, the vast majority of who went

to the United States. In 1860 38.93% of the foreign born population in the United States was Irish. In 1870, 33.3% of the foreign born population in the United States was Irish. The majority of Irish who went to the United States, came through New York. *The Famine Emigrants, 1846-1851*, edited by Ira A. Glazier should be referred to. Canada was the primary destination for the Irish in the period 1815 to 1850. Quebec City and Halifax were the major ports of entry until 1900.

The Australian Transportation records have been referred to above, subsequently money and land was offered to immigrants. Many emigration records are being placed on the Internet; go to the Famine and Emigration link at *www.IrishAncestors.net*.

Report of Irish Education Inquiry 1826
The appendix to the second report, contains details of all parochial schools and includes the names of teachers.

Ordnance Survey Memoirs 1830-1839
In 1824 a Committee set up by Parliament, recommended that a complete survey and valuation of Ireland be undertaken. The purpose of the survey was to redefine townland boundaries and, by a national valuation of land and buildings, make the striking of the rate more equitable.

The Memoirs were written descriptions intended to accompany the maps. Heads of Inquiry were stipulated under which information was to be reported, and this included topics of social as well as economic interest. The Memoirs covered the counties of Antrim, Armagh, Derry, Donegal, Fermanagh, and Tyrone. Manuscript material relating to the Memoirs is to be found in the Royal Irish Academy and the National Archives. The Institute of Irish Studies at the Queen's University of Belfast in association with the Royal Irish Academy has published a number of volumes of the Memoirs. The give an indication of the lives of the ordinary people.

Ordnance Survey Letters 1834-1841
John O'Donovan, who is best known for having edited the Annals of the Four Masters was employed by the Ordnance Survey, to ascertain accurately the old Irish names for townlands, villages, etc. In each area he collected historical information, he paid particular attention to surnames. The Ordnance Survey Letters were written, mostly by John O'Donovan between March 1834 and September 1841, they do not cover Antrim, Cork or Tyrone. His comments in the form of letters, which he sent to Dublin, have been typed in bookform for each county. These letters are available in the National Library of Ireland, in the Gilbert Library Dublin and the

County Libraries should have copies for their own area. A number of county volumes have now been published.

Return of Voters 1830-1840
The return of voters registered in each borough, stating names and address's is contained in volume 11 of the Reports from Committees (Parl. Papers) 1837.

Tenants Under £5 1837
The names and addresses of tenants holding tenements under £5 yearly value are also in above.

Commissioners of Public Instruction 1835
This report lists the names of teachers by parishes.

Incumbered Estate Records 1837-96
In the aftermath of the Famine, the Government established the Incumbered Estate Court to deal with bankrupt estates. The petitioner before the court had to prepare details of the estates, including the tenancies. During the period 1850-58, 8,000 estates were sold and information on such estates had to be prepared.

The National Archives has, a set of Incumbered Estate Court and Landed Estate Court Rentals. There are 148 volumes with indexes for the years 1850 -85. The Public Records Office in Belfast has, 83 volumes of printed rentals of the encumbered Estate Court for the years 1849 - 58. The National Library of Ireland has records for the years 1837-96 and there is an index covering the years 1850-64.

Poor Law Records 1838-1848
Poor law records are the archives of the Boards of Guardians who administered the poor law in Ireland from 1838 to 1948. The admission and discharge registers list those entering and leaving the workhouse; there are registers of births and deaths and of those receiving outdoor relief. All these records provide lists of names, which could well prove useful, particularly for the poor who are unlikely to be recorded elsewhere. There were also infirmaries and fever hospitals attached to the workhouses and there are lists of inmates available. The records for the 27 Poor Law Unions that covered the six counties are available in the Public Records Office in Belfast.

School Records
In 1831 National School were established by the Government. School registers may contain the following information: name, age, date of entry, parent's names, their address and occupation. The National Archives has some such records. The Records of the Commissioners for National Education, covering the period 1831 - 1922 provide a record of payments to teachers.

Royal Irish Constabulary 1836-1922
The Irish Constabulary was established in 1836 (becoming 'Royal" in September 1867). The Dublin Metropolitan Police being separate. These records normally give full name, age, height, religious affiliations, native county, trade or calling, marital status, native county of wife, date of appointment, counties in which served, length of service and date of retirement or death. The original of these records are at the British Public Records Office in Kew. The National Archives, Public Records Office in Belfast, the RUC Museum in Lisburn and LDS Library have these records on microfilm.

Papal Army Volunteers 1860
The Unification of Italy threatened the temporal power of the Pope in the Papal States, this encouraged many Irish to join the Papal Army. The 59th Report of the Deputy Keeper of Public Records at pages 85-105, contains the names and addresses of Irish volunteers for the Papal Army 1860.

British Army Records
Many of the service records of soldiers who were in the British Army are at the British Public Records Office in Kew. From the mid-eighteenth century a considerable amount may be discovered about army ancestors. *Military Records for Genealogists* published by the British Public Records Office should be consulted.

Return of the owners of land 1876
An outcome of confiscations of Irish land was the creation of very large estates. A list of landowners was published in 1876: Return of owners of land of one acre and upwards, in the several counties, counties of cities, and counties of towns in Ireland, to which is added a summary for each province and for all Ireland, it has been re-published by the Genealogical Publishing Company (1970), it is also on CD-Rom. There were 19 estates of between 50,000 and 160,000 acres, 254 estates of between 10,000 and 50,000 acres and 418 estates of between 5,000 and 10,000 acres. The large family estates were finally broken up under the Land Acts and the Incumbered Estates Court.

Land Purchase Acts 1885 1903 1923

The Land Commission, which was established in 1881, in 1885, was given powers in relation to land purchase. Money was advanced to tenants under the various Acts to purchase their holdings. The Commission had to satisfy themselves as to the ability of the tenant to repay the annuities. Inspectors traveled the countryside and reports were drawn up. The Schedule of Tenancies is a record of the sitting tenants on the estate at the time of purchase and is accompanied by a reference map.

Estate Records

The outcome of all the confiscations, plantations and settlement of Ireland was the survival of some great medieval and later plantation estates. The Lands Acts and the Incumbered Estates Court finally broke up these estates. The collections of estate records may contain the following:

Rent rolls: which normally list the tenants by townland;

Leases: which give the tenants name and perhaps those of his children, with their ages.

Rent ledgers: showing what each tenant had to pay in rent;

Maps: which plot tenants holdings on a scale of about 6' to 1 mile;

Wages books: will contain the names of labourers, servants and gardeners who may not be tenants;

Land agents notebooks: may contain details of a tenant and his family;

Land agents letters: may refer to persons on the estate or in the area.

If you do not know the name of a local landlord, you may be able to find it from the Primary Valuation (see chapter 5).

Directories and Almanacs

It was common, particularly during the Nineteenth Century for town directories to be issued. The earliest directories confine themselves to merchants and traders the later ones list all householders. All directories should be available in the National Library of Ireland and a good selection is available in the Public Records Office. The County Libraries too should have directories covering their own area.

Newspapers

It was the practice in the past, as well as at the present time for notices of birth, marriage and death to appear in the newspapers. The National Library of Ireland has the best available collection of Irish newspapers. The oldest dating from February 1660. All newspapers pertaining to Ireland are now being placed on microfilm by the National Library Microfilm Unit. This work is part of the NEWSPLAN project, which is drawing upon resources through the British Isles. A list of Irish newspapers available on microfilm may be downloaded from the website of the National Library. The British Library in London also has Irish newspapers. The County Libraries should also be inquired of. The Public Records Office in Belfast has produced a booklet in conjunction with the Library Association on the availability of northern newspapers from 1737 to the present time. For relevant links go to Newspapers at *www.IrishAncestors.net.*

Gravestone inscriptions
A visit to a local cemetery may provide some genealogical information, and will certainly give an indication of the surnames in a locality. The recognition of particular Christian name, or group of Christian names in a family may be an indication of a distant relative and the present families could then be located.

Most families could not have been able to afford a headstone in the past, so the likelihood is that no information may be obtainable. Many older headstones have been weathered and will prove difficult to read. Information obtained from gravestones has been published, mostly in local historical journals.

Register of Electors
The register of electors, which is revised annual, could prove a useful genealogical tool. It can help a person locate those who may be distantly related to themselves. Sections of the register for a particular area are available at local libraries, post offices and police stations.

Ireland Memorial Record 1914 - 1918
This lists the names of Irish soldiers who died in the British Army during the Great War. The information given consists of name, date of death, hometown and regiment. The Gilbert Library has a copy.

Free Citizens of Dublin
From 1192 until 1918, admission to the "Freedom of the City of Dublin" meant that one was entitled to vote in municipal and parliamentary elections. The Freedom of the City was confined to a restricted group of people, in general to qualify it was necessary to have been born within the city boundaries, those who were "of the Irish Nation" were excluded.

Amongst the categories of admission to the freedom of the city were:

Service: Once an apprentice had completed service to a master in one of the Trade Guilds of Dublin, and had been admitted to full membership of the Guild, application could be made.

Birth: The sons of Freemen were entitled to apply for admission, usually after the death of their father.

Marriage: Marriage to a woman who held the Freedom in her own right, or to the daughter of a freeman, entitled a husband to make application.

Fine: Prosperous professional men, or tradesmen who were not members of a Trade Guild, could make application on payment of money.

Act of Parliament: Many Huguenots made application under an Act of 1662, which was passed to "encourage Protestant Strangers to Settle in Ireland".

The lists of the Free Citizens of Dublin contain in the region of 45,000 names and it is possible to trace several generations of old Dublin families through such lists.

United States Social Security Death Index

This lists all the people in the United States who had social security numbers and who died since 1962. It can be purchased on CD-Rom and is accessible via the Internet. Click Online Ancestral Search at *www.IrishAncestors.net*.

In addition the following maybe consulted:

> Court Records
> Military, Naval and Police Records
> Local History Society Journals
> Heritage Centres
> Parliamentary Records
> Government Records
> Memoriam Cards

Chapter 8

National Library of Ireland

This is located beside Leinster House on Kildare Street, Dublin 2.
Tel: +353 (0)1 603 0200; Fax: 676 6690; *www.nli.ie* .
The main reading room is open as follows:

Monday - Wednesday	10 a.m. to 9 p.m.
Thursday - Friday	10 a.m. to 5 p.m.
Saturday	10 a.m. to 1 p.m.

Genealogical advisory service

The National Library does not offer a research service to readers or correspondents. However a free genealogical advisory service is available to personal callers. Library staff provide inquirers with an outline of relevant sources available in Irish and other repositories, and direct them towards source material in the National Library. If a person has time there is no reason not to take advantage of this service.

Readers's ticket

A reader's ticket is required to use the library. Application for a reader's ticket (which may be issued for up to five years) can be made on entry and there is no difficulty when required for genealogical purposes. You are required to sign the register at the service counter each day as you enter. If you use the manuscript reading room you must also sign the register there.

Using the National Library

Having signed the register, one should seat oneself at a table. During the summer a person may have to wait until a table becomes available. In order to obtain books or other materials, a call slip must be filled out. These are available at the service counter and you are asked not to fill out more that three at any one time. The call number will be found in the appropriate catalogue.

If the subject volumes of the printed book catalogue are consulted under a particular county or under whatever village, town, or parish you are interested in you will find any book or pamphlets required. Items acquired since 1968 are listed in a separate card catalogue.

Materials are issued to readers at their tables generally within five to fifteen minutes. When leaving the library (apart from absences of up to fifteen minutes) materials should be returned to the service counter and you should retrieve your call slips, this is your proof that you have returned what material was brought to you.

Photocopying facilities by the following processes are available: xerox, photograph, microfilm, printout from microfilm. Details and charges are displayed on a notice board in the printed books reading room.

The records
The genealogical sources in the National Library are numerous and reference is made to them continually in the other chapters of this book. What follows can only be a brief account of what is contained in this repository.

Printed material
The National Library is a copyright library for both Ireland and Britain, and as such it has copies of all books published during the past hundred years or so. It follows that the library has copies of all printed sources. This includes a complete series of archeological and historical journals, to which there is a card index (which has been microfilmed). It has the largest and most complete collection of regional, county, parish and town histories. There are also numerous family histories and published genealogies.

Microfilms
The library has been active in acquiring microfilms of all records of Irish interest from manuscripts in libraries and archives in Ireland and abroad. The Report of the Council of Trustees contains details on accessions of microfilms. Much of the material on microfilm in the National Library is referred to elsewhere. Collections from various archives have been microfilmed; including the Office of the Chief Herald, Trinity College Dublin, the Friends' Library, and the Registry of Deeds.

Catholic parish registers
Roman Catholic Parish records on microfilm, which have been considered in Chapter 4.

Primary Valuation
The Primary Valuation of Rateable Property in Ireland edited by Richard Griffith, which has been considered in Chapter 5 is here.

Surname's index
The index to surnames in the Primary Valuation and the Tithe Books is here. There is a volume for each county.

Lists of Electors
Freeholders who satisfied a property requirement were entitled to vote.
There are several of these lists in the library: consult Subject Catalogue
under "Elections".

Directories
General directories are on open access; among these there is a good
collection of Dublin directories from about 1730 and a complete file of
Thom's Almanac and Official Directory from 1844. Directories relating to
individual towns or counties will be located through the Subject Catalogue
of printed books.
Most towns are included in the following:
Pigot, City of Dublin and Hibernian Provincial Directory (1824);
Slater, National Commercial Directory of Ireland (1846 to 1894;
MacDonald, Irish Directory and Gazetteer (from 1902 to 1955).
Pigot and Slater give general information on towns and large villages and
have lists of gentry, professionals, farmers, traders and tradesmen.

Ordnance Survey Books and Letters
The Ordnance Survey letters of John O'Donovan and the name books
consisting of topographical and antiquarian data on townlands, towns and
parishes are here. There are transcript copies available, arranged by
county. There are also copies available on microfilm.
The Ordnance Survey letters for a number of counties have now been
published in separate volumes.

Newspapers
There are newspapers files from the seventeenth century onwards, but
mainly covering the nineteenth century and the twentieth century. There is
a catalogue available which contains an alphabetical list of newspapers
with details of holdings in hardcopy or microfilm. There is an index of
publication and there is also a table showing titles available for each
decade back to 1680. To find a newspaper published in the locality that you
are interested in, consult the Newspaper List. It has a list of provincial
papers arranged by place of publication and details of the National
Library's file for each title.

Estate papers and records
The estate papers and records which have been considered in chapter 7
are here. A list and indexes of estate records in the Irish Land Commission
(the originals of which are not available for consultation) is also here.

There is a list of reports on manuscript collections in private keeping, reference to which is made in *Analecta Hibernica* numbers 20 and 23.

Maps

The first edition (1833-46) of six-inch Ordnance Survey maps, with revised editions for particular counties from 1855 to 1893 are here. A revised edition on a larger scale (1/2,500) was begun after 1887. Also there are large scale plans of towns, mainly five-foot, published in the second half of the nineteenth century.

There is a map catalogue which includes printed and manuscript maps. Entries are arranged alphabetically by places and person; check all the entries relating to the particular county, as well as those relating to the specific locality that you are interested in.

Wills

The library has on microfilm the wills indexes to grantors and to lands in the Registry of Deeds. A list and indexes of wills in the Irish Land Commission (the originals of which are not available for consultation) are available. A great deal of information in relation to wills has been published and such publications are available here.

Manuscripts

To find out what is available consult the places volumes of *Manuscript Sources for the History of Irish Civilization* (edited by R. J. Hayes 1965). A supplement covering the period 1965-75 has been published, while a card catalogue of material processed since 1975 is available for consultation in the manuscript reading room. Entries are arranged by persons, subjects, places, dates and in the case of materials that are not in the National Library of Ireland, by institutions. With regard to places, entries are arranged by county with place within county in alphabetical order; you should check all entries for the county that you are interested in.

British Parliamentary Papers

These cover the period from the Act of Union, often termed "Blue Books". Many of these publications such as reports of Parliamentary committees and commissions have substantial material of a local nature included in minutes of evidence and appendices.

Office of the Chief Herald

The Office of the Chief Herald is the Office of Arms for Ireland. This office is a department of the National Library, and is located at 2 Kildare Street, Dublin 2.

It is not a public office, is not open to the public for genealogical work, and has no facilities for the public to search. A house researcher is available to undertake searches on behalf of the public in the records of the office. Such searches are charged at the rate of £50 per hour.

The Office of Arms was established during the reign of Henry VII in 1552 and the person in charge of the office was known as "Ulster King of Arms". The first "Ulster" was Bartholomew Butler and many of those who have held this office contributed to the availability of genealogical source material.

Coats of arms

The function of the office, in the past as it is today, is to confirm and grant coats of arms (A practice which in a republic has no basis in law). Coats of arms were granted under Royal Authority to a male individual and his male heirs. The fact that another individual may have the same surname is merely coincidental and gives no right to claim a coat of arms. Heraldry had no place in Gaelic Ireland, the Normans brought it into Ireland and the Septs had not got coats of arms. It is unfortunate that the commercial exploitation of heraldry has caused confusion. The term "Genealogical Office" which it was renamed in 1943 (after being transferred from British to Irish administration) is a misnomer, as it is clearly the office of the "Chief Herald of Ireland."

Given the importance of pedigrees in its work the Office of Arms naturally accumulated a vast amount of genealogical material. Unfortunately this pertains mostly to influential families of past centuries and there may not be much of importance to the majority of Irish people.

The records

Amongst the record here (the most important of which are on microfilm and available for consultation in the National Library):

The register of Grants of Arms dating from 1552.

The pedigree charts made by Sir William Bentham, from his abstract of the prerogative wills.

Abstracts of all Prerogative Administrations Intestate down to 1800, also made by Bentham.

Abstracts of the Prerogative Marriage Licences (1630 to 1858).

Collection of obituaries from 18th century newspapers compiled by T.U. Sadlier.

Extracts from the Chancery and Exchequer pleadings made by
   W.H. Welply.

Abstracts from wills, the originals of which did not survive. These wills
   are indexed by name, address, and year, which index was published
   in Analecta Hibernica No. 17 (1949)

Funeral Certificates, which date from 1588 to 1729 and contain a return
   of the names, parentage, arms, marriage, issue, date and place of
   burial, of those whose funerals were attended by "Ulster".

Inquisitions Post Mortmen, transcripts for Munster and Connaught,

Abstract of grants under the Acts of Settlement and Explanation,
   1666 - 1684.

Transcript of the Heart Money Rolls 1666, considered in ch. 8.

Linea Antiqua, a manuscript by Roger O'Ferrall dated 1709,
   which contains genealogical information on many Gaelic families.

Copies of the Religious Census 1766 for parts of Ireland,

Poll Books and lists of Freeholders from various counties in various
   years, "Alphabetical List of the Freeholders of the City of Dublin
   and their place of abode, and of the Freemen of the twenty-five
   corporations" which was published in 1768.

Army and Militia Lists covering various counties, for the late
   eighteenth century.

Transcript of Census Records, which were destroyed.

Chapter 9

The National Archives

The Public Records Office of Ireland was established by the Public Records (Ireland) Act 1867 under a Deputy Keeper of Records. Since 1892 the same person always held the two posts of Deputy Keeper of Public Records and Keeper of State Paper's, but the two departments continued a separate existence. The National Archives Act 1986 created a new institution, known as the National Archives, to take over the functions of the State Paper Office and the Public Record Office, with a Director of the National Archives in charge.

The National Archives are now located at Bishop Street, Dublin 8. Telephone: +353 (0)1 407 2300; Fax: 407 2333.
www.nationalarchives.ie/genealogy.html

The reading room is open: Monday to Friday 10 am to 5 pm it does not close for lunch but service is suspended (12.45 pm to 2 pm). Documents will be produced during the hours of 10 am to 1 pm and 2 pm to 4.30 pm. Dockets must be placed in the tray before 12.45 pm for production before lunch and before 4.30 pm for production in the afternoon.

A reader's ticket is required to search through the records, but there is no difficulty in obtaining such for genealogical research. These are now issued on a calendar year basis.

A photocopying service is available and fees are displayed in the reading room.

Annual reports

The Deputy Keeper of Records, under the provisions of the 1867 Act, was required to publish an annual report regarding the work of classifying and arranging the records, the nature of the accessions, and an index to the documents by name, date, classification, and location which were not included in the larger collections with their own indexes. The *Reports of the Deputy Keeper of the Public Records of Ireland* were published annually between 1869 and 1921. However only six Reports were published from 1926 to 1962. They comprise 59 volumes with appendices, including indexes.

In 1922 there was a fire in the Public Records Office and many records were lost. After the fire, appeals were made in Ireland or abroad, for all those who had copied the records in the past, to send their copies or transcripts, abstracts, or notes, to replace the burned records. Much valuable work has been done to replace the lost records.

The 55th to the 58th Reports of the Deputy Keeper published between 1928 and 1951, furnish information as to the collections that have been accumulated, indexed and are available to the public. A *Short Guide to the Public Records Office of Ireland* (1964) by Griffith is an introduction to the National Archives. This is out of print, however a photocopy is on sale at the reading room desk.

The Reading Room
There are published works of a genealogical nature on the open shelves:
>   Reports of the Deputy Keeper
>   Manuscript Sources for the History of Irish Civilization
>   Townland Index
>   Census Reports 1821-
>   The Irish Manuscripts Commission publications
>   Analecta Hibernica
>   Parish Registers
>   Index to Wills
>   Memorial of the Dead
>   Graveyard Inscriptions
>   Thom's Directory.

Indexes
There are also in the reading room card catalogues and typed indexes to the various collections, which are of great assistance in locating the record that is being sought.
These are as follows:
>   Annual Calendar of Wills and Administrations
>   Judgments and Orders
>   Marriage Licence Bonds
>   Carte Transcripts
>   Crossle Genealogical Abstract
>   Jennings Notes
>   Thrift Genealogical Abstracts
>   Maps and Rentals (names and places)
>   Wills Extracts in Office of Charitable Donations
>   Proclamations (names and places)
>   Miscellaneous Records
>   Index of Surnames in Primary Valuation and Tithe Books
>   Shipping Records Names
>   National Schools by county then name of school
>   Pre-1708 Deeds by county then barony
>   A "Nineteenth Century Census" list
>   Finding Aids

In addition the shelves in the reading room contain folders that act as finding aids to the sources. Here will be found the reference number to the record to be sought. This reference number is written on a docket, which is placed in a tray. The record will then be brought to you.

The Records

As the State repository the National Archives has a great amount of material of a genealogical nature. Many of the records in the National Archives are discussed in other chapters and it is only necessary to make brief reference here.

Accordingly among the records that may be consulted are:

Census returns, complete for 1901/1911, discussed in Chapter 2;

Church of Ireland parish registers, discussed in Chapter 4;

The Primary Valuation, discussed in Chapter 5;

The Tithe Books, discussed in Chapter 6;

Betham's genealogical abstracts containing more information than the pedigrees in the Office of the Chief Herald;

Marriage Licence Bonds for the Church of Ireland covering the period 1650 to 1845; Chancery and Equity Bills;

Records of the Land Commission, Valuation Office and Quit Rent Office;

Wills

During the period prior to 1857, the ecclesiastical courts of the Church of Ireland had jurisdiction in relation to wills. Each diocese had a Consistorial Court, it was this court that granted probate. If a deceased had property of more than £5 in a second diocese, then the matter had to go to the Prerogative Court, which was under the jurisdiction of the Archbishop of Armagh. The Probate Act (Ireland) 1857 abolished the jurisdiction of the ecclesiastical courts. It established a principal registry in Dublin and eleven district registries.

The records of wills and administration now in the National Archives include the following:

(a) Original wills and administration papers lodged in the Principal Registry since 1904, and in most District Registries since 1900 (indexed in the annual Calendars).

(b) Will books containing copies of most wills proved in District Registries since 1858, and of some wills proved in the Principal Registry in 1874, 1876, 1891 and 1896 (indexed in the annual Calendars).

(c) Grant books containing copies of grants made in the Principal Registry since 1922 and in 1878, 1883, 1891 and 1893, and of most grants made in the District Registries since 1858 (indexed in the annual Calendars)

(d) Betham's abstracts of wills proved in the Prerogative Court before 1800, of administrations granted in the Prerogative Court before 1802, and of wills proved in the Kildare Diocesan Court before 1827 (indexed in Vicar's Index, the Indexes to Prerogative Grants, and the Index to Wills of the Diocese of Kildare reprinted from the Journal of Kildare Archaeological Society, iv, no. 6. (1905)

(e) Inland Revenue registers of wills and administrations, 1828-39 (indexed in separate indexes which cover the period 1828-79; for the years 1840-57 these indexes give details which do not appear in the general indexes referred to above)

(f) Charitable Donations and Bequests will extract books containing abstracts of wills that made charitable bequests, 1800-1961 (there is a separate card index for the period 1800-58)

(g) Other copies and abstracts of wills and administrations for the periods both before and after 1858 (indexed in the main testamentary card index)

State Paper Office

The State Paper Office is now a sub-office of the National Archives Most of the documents relate to the administration of Ireland during the years 1790 to 1922. The classes of State Papers are as follows:

Records of the Chief Secretary's office:

> Westmoreland correspondence 1789-1808
> Rebellion papers 1790-1807
> State of the country papers 1790-1831
> Official papers 1790-1922
> Registered papers (incl. outrage paper) 1818-1924
> Letter books 1801-1912

Police and crime records:

> Irish crime records 1848-93
> Fenian papers 1857-83
> Crime branch special records 1887-1920
> Police records 1848-1921

Records of the department of Chief Secretary's office:

> Convict prisons office 1836-80
> Privy council office 1800-1922
> Chief Crown Solicitors's department 1815-1922

General prison board:

> Government prisons office 1936-80
> Office of inspector-general of prisons 1836-80
> General prisons board 1877-1928

Transportation Records 1791-1853

Convicts transported to Australia in the first half of the 19th Century numbered approximately 40,000. The documents relating to such transportation were microfilmed as a Bicentennial gift to Australia. The transportation records are considered in detail in chapter 7.

Chapter 10

Public Records Office Belfast

This is located at 66 Balmoral Avenue, Belfast BT9 6NY.
Tel: + 44 (0)28 90 255905; Fax: 255999; *www.proni.nics.gov.uk*.
E-mail: proni@dcalni.gov.uk

It is open to the public Monday to Friday 9.15 a. m. to 4.45 p. m. (8.45 p.m. on Thursdays) and does not close for lunch. There is a canteen on the complex, which may be used by visitors. It closes for two weeks in late November/early December for stocktaking.

This repository was opened in March 1924. It houses the most complete collection of genealogical, legal and historical records in relation to Ulster (the records are not confined to the six counties). Starting from scratch in 1924, it is no exaggeration to say that; there has been accumulated as much genealogical material as is housed in the National Archives and the National Library of Ireland.

The Public Records Office in Belfast is an excellent facility and contrasts very seriously with the state of access to genealogical sources in Dublin. The many records that have been accumulated are listed and indexed in the Reports of the Deputy Keeper. In addition this office has published many books and pamphlets to guide one in genealogical research.

Access
On arrival you must fill in your full name and permanent address in the attendance book in the reception hall. You will need a reader's ticket, which will be issued to you on completion of a reader's application form stating the subject and purpose of your research. There is no difficulty when required for genealogical purposes. The reader's ticket is valid for onc calendar year.

A photocopying service is available. The costs vary according to the size of the document, the complexity of the order and the type of copy required.

Indexes and typescript catalogues
The public search room is very spacious and well laid out, it contains three extensive card indexes and bound typescript catalogues of all the listed collections of documents in the office.

The card indexes are not a direct index to documents. They direct the searcher to the appropriate typescript catalogue.

Personal Names Index: This index contains the names of individuals mentioned in many of the original documents.

Place Names Index: This is arranged alphabetically.

Subject Index: This covers specific subjects, such as the linen industry.

The typescript catalogue enables you to decide which documents will be useful in your search, and worth ordering from the stores. The reference number is obtained from the typescript catalogue.

Sectional lists give a brief summary of certain categories of documents and, like the card index; they give references, which direct you to the typescript catalogues.

Such lists are available for:

> Textile industry records
>
> Landed estate records
>
> Church registers
>
> Maps and plans

Colored bindings are used to distinguish the catalogues of the various categories of records.

> Brown: Official records of Government and local authorities
>
> Black: Parish registers
>
> Blue: Original privately deposited papers
>
> Red: Photocopies of privately deposited papers
>
> Green: Microfilm copies

Private collections are referenced as follows:

> D: an original document
>
> T: a transcript or photocopy
>
> MIC: a microfilm copy
>
> CR: church records

Getting a document

Fill in a request form, giving the full reference number and a seat number in the reading room. Hand in the form at the issue desk and the document will be brought to you. The length of time that you may have to wait varies and may be up to 45 minutes.

Reference books

Standard reference books on the search room shelves are also available for use in addition to the catalogues and lists.

Records

Many of the records in the Public Records Office are discussed in other chapters and it is only necessary to make brief reference here. Accordingly among the records that may be consulted are:

Census returns on microfilm for 1901 the six counties (See Chapter 2);

Civil registration, index to births registered in the whole of Ireland (1864 -1922), also the original registers of birth and death for the six counties, discussed in Chapter 3;

Church of Ireland parish registers, discussed in Chapter 4, also Vestry Records, a *Guide to Church Records* may be consulted;

The Primary Valuation, discussed in Chapter 5;

The Tithe Books, discussed in Chapter 6;

Wills, which are discussed in Chapters 8, 9 and 12:

There is an index to pre-1858 wills: 1536 to 1810 for all Ireland and from 1811 to 1857 for the six counties;

The Yearly Calendars to Wills and Administrations from 1858 are on the open shelves;

There is also a consolidated index for the years 1858-77 which is being completed up to 1900;

Original wills and administration papers lodged in Belfast and Derry and most of those lodged in Armagh, which cover Ulster (excluding Cavan) but includes part of Louth;

Will books for Armagh, Belfast and Derry;

Grant books Armagh, Belfast and Derry.

Ordnance survey maps

Ordnance survey letters of John O'Donovan;

Hearth Money, Subsidy and Poll Tax Records;

Militia, Yeomanry and Muster Records;

Voters, Poll and Freeholders Records;

Landed Estate Records;

Poor Law Records;

County and Grand Jury Records;

Emigration Records;

Seventeenth Century Survey Records (The Books of Survey and Distribution);

Betham's genealogical abstracts;

Marriage Licence Bonds (1650 to 1845);

Pedigrees and genealogical papers;

National school records

Gravestone inscriptions.

Chapter 11

Office of the Registrar-General Dublin

This is located at Joyce House 8/11 East Lombard Street, Dublin 2.
Tel: + 353 (0)1 635 4000; *www.groireland.ie*

The search room is open to the public Monday to Friday 9.30 am to 4.30 pm and is closed 12.30 pm to 2.15 pm for lunch. A project is ongoing since 1996, to electronically capture and store registration data as images and index data on a database. It is expected that this will be completed by late 2002. It is planned that there be access to records via the Internet.

Fees

As of the 2nd November 1987 (still current at June 2002) the fees payable by the public are as follows:

Certificates of Birth or Marriage £5.50 (€ 6.98), additional copies £4.00 (€ 5.08).

Short certificate of Birth £3.50 (€ 4.44), additional copy £2.00 (€2.54).

Certificate of Death £3.00? (€ 6.98).

Particular search £1.50 (€ 1.90)

A search through any indexes over any period not exceeding five years for any given entry

General search £12.00 (€ 15.24)

A search through the indexes without specifying the object of the search

Photocopy of a specified entry in the register £1.50 (€ 1.90)

Searching

The fee, which you must pay, gives an entitlement to search through the indexes only. You may not search through the registers, and it is not possible get sight of the actual registers here. You must give a reference number, obtainable from the indexes, and receive a photocopy of what is contained in the register.

There is a small search room with tables and all the indexes are in that room. There are shelves containing many volumes, which index alphabetically all the entries contained in the registers. There is at least one clerk on duty to obtain your photocopy requests.

Civil registration has already been considered in Chapter 3 and reference should be made to that chapter.

Registers and Records deposited in Registrar-General's Office

1. Registers of Births registered in all Ireland on and after 1st January 1864 to 31st December 1921, and in Ireland (exclusive of the six north eastern counties) from that date.

2. Registers of Deaths, registered in all Ireland on and after 1st January 1864 to 31st December 1921, and in Ireland (exclusive of the six north eastern counties) from that date.

3. Registers of Marriages in all Ireland from 1st April 1845 to 31st December 1863 except those celebrate by the Roman Catholic Clergy.

4. Registers of all Marriages registered in the whole of Ireland on and after the 1st January 1864 to 31st December 1921 and in Ireland (exclusive of the six north eastern counties) from that date.

5. Registers of Births at Sea of Children, one of whose parents is Irish, registered since 1st January 1864 to 31st December 1921, and after that date, of children of Irish parentage, not including children of parents belonging to the six north eastern counties.

6. Registers of Deaths at Sea of Irish born persons, registered since 1st January 1864 to 31st December 1921, and after that date of Irish born persons other than those born in the six north eastern counties.

7. Registers of Births of Children of Irish parents, certified by British Consuls abroad, since 1st January 1864 to 31st December 1921.

8. Registers of Deaths of Irish born persons certified by British Consuls abroad, since 1st. January 1864 to 31st December 1921.

9. Registers of Marriages celebrated in Dublin by the late Rev. J.G.F. Schulze, Minister of the German Protestant Church, Poolbeg Street, Dublin from 1806 to 1837 inclusive.

10. Registers under the "Births, Deaths, and Marriages (Army) Act 1879".

11. Original Certificates of Marriages celebrated by the Roman Catholic Clergy from 1st January 1864 to 30th September 1881 (The Registration of Marriages (Ireland) Act 1863 Section 11).

13. Adopted Children Register - legal adoptions registered on or after 10th July 1953.

14. Birth and Death registers under the Defence (Amendment) Act (No. 2) 1960.

15. Register of certain Births and Deaths occurring outside the State (The Births, Deaths and Marriages Registration Act 1972 Section 4).

16. Register of certain Lourdes Marriages (Marriages Act 1972, section 2)

Office of the Registrar-General Belfast

This office is located at Oxford House, 49/55 Chichester Street, Belfast BT1 4HL. Tel: + 44 (0)28 90 252000; *www.groni.gov.uk/index.htm*
There is an online and telephone service for certificates, gro.nisra@dfpni.gov.uk.

The office is open to the public: Monday to Friday from 9.30 am to 4.00 pm and it does not closed for lunch.
The principal records in the Office of the Registrar-General are:
Indexes of Births, Marriages and Deaths (all Ireland 1845-64-1922)
Registers of Births and Deaths registered in the six counties from 1st January 1864. Registers of Marriages registered in the Six Counties from 1922. The registers of Marriages prior to 1922 are in local custody.
As of the 1st November 1998 the fees payable are as follows:

> Certificates of Birth, Death or Marriage £7.00 (£4.00).
> Short certificate of Birth £7.00 (£4.00)

Searches -

> Five year search £3.00
> Index search £6.00
> Assisted search £15.00

There is at the present time a three months waiting list for searches and one may telephone, or call in, to make an appointment. The office will usually take only one researcher a day. Due to staff holidays no researching is allowed during the summer.

Access to registers

The fee, which a person must pay in Dublin, gives an entitlement to search through the indexes only but not through the register. It is not possible here to get actual sight of the register; you must give a reference number and receive a photocopy (at a fee of £1.50 for each entry) of what is contained in the register. In order not to waste money a person would have to be certain of anything found in the index.

In Belfast, you also search through the indexes. On been give a reference number, the staff will then read out the information in the entry to you. They will not allow you to see the entry. Fortunately, a person is not confined to going to the Belfast or Dublin offices to get access to the indexes or sight of the registers. You have the option to search through the microfilm indexes in the LDS Family History Centres. Subsequently a person may then get a photocopy of an entry in Dublin or obtain details of an entry in Belfast, or visit the local registration office of the area that he or she may be interested in.

Chapter 12

Registry of Deeds

This is located in the Kings Inns, Henrietta Street, Dublin 7.
Telephone: + 353 (0)1 670 7500; LoCall 1890 333001.
www.gov.ie/landreg/registry_of_deeds_services.htm

It is open from: Monday to Friday from 10 am to 4.30 pm. All information relating to the period prior to 1833 must be sought out by attending the office in person. The public may inspect the records on payment of € 6.00 for each name for each period of ten years or part thereof.

King John introduced the common law of England into Ireland. Feudal law provided that the King was owner of all land, he made grants of land in return for services and duties renderable. These grantees in turn made grants of land to lesser people on similar terms. In course of time "secret deeds" were devised to transfer land outside the feudal system.

The Registry of Deeds was established from 1708 in order to facilitate people who wished to register their ownership of land and to outlaw the practice of "secret deeds". The Registration of Deeds Act 1707 stated its purpose as: " for securing purchasers, preventing forgeries and fraudulent gifts and conveyances of lands, tenements and hereditaments, which have been frequently practised in this kingdom, especially by Papists, to the great prejudice of the Protestant interest thereof."

Records
The records are intact from 1708; they have been neither lost or destroyed. The deeds (documents) registered consisted of: conveyances of freehold property, Assignment of leases, mortgages, marriage settlements and wills. In 1832 an Act was passed which in practice limited registration to deeds affecting lands. Prior to the Land Acts at the end of the nineteenth century most farms were held as yearly tenancies or short term leases and as such were considered not to come within the provisions of the Act, which exempted dwelling-houses for terms under twenty-one years from registration. Dwelling houses were usually held under short-term tenancies, it can be taken that records of transactions affecting such tenancies are unlikely to exist in the Registry of Deeds.

Memorial of the Deed
The memorial is a synopsis of the origional deed consisting of particulars complying with the 1707 Act. The memorials contain the following details: the date of the deed, conveyance or will, the names and addresses of all the parties, of all the witnesses and all the lands and their situation. From 1st January 1930 these are on microfilm. On registration of a Deed,

which is returned to the solicitor at the time of registration, the memorial of the deed is retained, given a reference number and indexed in the Names Index and prior to 1947 in the Lands Index.

Transcript Books 1708-1960
Memorial were fully transcribed and copied into books. However not all memorials were copied.

Abstract Book 1833-
These are a summary of the memorial; they are manual from 1833, and on computer from 1st January 1980. A copy of an abstract or print out of an abstract gives: the reference (Year, Book No.), date of registration, name and date of instrument, the names of the Grantor and one Grantee, consideration (if any), the description of the property, and general nature of the instrument.

Index of Grantors / Names Index
This is manual from 1708 to 1979, on microfilm from 1708 to date, and on computer from 1st January 1980. In the Names Index the reference number to the memorial is indexed under the surname of the party or parties granting (the grantor) and shows the first grantee and from 1832 the county or city affected is listed.

Index of Lands / Lands Index (1709-1946)
In the Lands Index the reference number to the memorial was indexed in volumes assigned to each county, city, or corporate town. The name of a townland in a county or of a street in a city or town, with the name of the first Grantor and Grantee. References to Abstract Book and Transcript Book are given.
There is no alphabetical index to grantees. The National Library of Ireland has microfilm copies of the indexes.

Wills
Wills provide much genealogical information: they often contain references to several members of a family, giving their names and relationships to the deceased person. *Abstracts of Wills at the Registry of Deeds*, Vol I (1708-45) and Vol II (1746-85) edited by P.B. Eustace and Vol III (1785-1832) edited by E. Ellis and P.B. Eustace has been published. These volumes have indexes to testators, beneficiaries, witnesses and placenames.

To search for more recent wills reference should be made to the National Archives or the Public Records Office, Belfast.

Given the nature of land ownership in Ireland after the penal times most of the genealogical information to be obtained would relate to plantation families.

Chapter 13

Other Repositories of Records

Here are repositories of genealogical records in Ireland and elsewhere. Any of the institutions listed that have websites are linked to from *www.IrishAncestors.net*, which will provide up to date information. Information as to location, telephone numbers, opening and closing times and fees often change (what is here is current at June 2002). Given the Diaspora of the Irish, a genealogical search should not be confined to Irish records or searches in Ireland.

The Royal Irish Academy

The Royal Irish Academy is located at 19 Dawson Street, Dublin 2. Tel: + 353 (0) 1 6762570, 6764222, 6761642. *www.ria.ie*
It is open from 9.30 am to 5.30 pm Monday to Friday.

The Academy was established by royal charter in 1786. The library has amongst its collection the largest and most ancient genealogical manuscript collections, together with seventeenth century government records and much other miscellaneous genealogical source material in Ireland.

The Linen Hall Library

This is located at 17 Donegal Square North, Belfast BT1 5GD.
Tel: +44 (0)28 90 321707; Fax: 90 438586. *www.linenhall.com*
It is open from 9.30 am to 5.30 pm (closing at 4.00 pm Saturday). This library was founded in 1788 and has a very good local studies collection.

Irish Land Commission

The Records Branch is located in Bishop Street, Dublin 8. Tel: +353 (0)1 4750766. The documents in the Land Commission have been catalogued on a barony basis by estates. This catalogue as referred to above is available for inspection in the National Library of Ireland. The documentation concerns estates acquired under the various land acts and consists mostly of: Abstract of Title, Description of Estates, Inspectors Report, Surveyors Report and schedule of Tenancies.

Land Valuation Office

This is located at Irish Life Centre, Lower Abbey Street, Dublin 1.
Tel: +353 (0)1 817 1000; Locall 1890 304 444; Fax: 817 1180
www.valoff.ie/; E-mail info@valoff.ie.

It is open Monday to Friday 9.30 am to 4.30 pm (closed for lunch 12.30 pm to 2 pm). This office has the Primary Valuation for the twenty-six counties with accompanying maps. It has records of valuation since 1852, showing occupiers of property. The fees for archive research are € 3.81 for less than one hour, thereafter € 15.24 per hour.

Representative Church Body Library
This is the library of the Church of Ireland and is located at Braemor Park, Rathgar, Dublin 6. Tel: + 353 (0)1 492 3979; Fax: 492 4770. *www.ireland.anglican.org/library/libroots.html*;
E-mail library@ireland.anglican.org.
It is open from 9.30 am to 4.45 pm Monday to Friday.
This library holds records of 600 parishes. In addition it holds biographical succession lists of clergy; collections of copy wills; extracts from the religious census of 1766; and collections of pedigrees.
Original pre-1870 parish registers (though still public records) which were retained in local custody have been collected here. Transcripts of the parish registers in the National Archives have been made and are here, together with transcripts made prior to 1922 by Tenison Groves. The library has on microfilm, records in other repositories. The *Irish Genealogist* (1982-) published biennially is a guide to the parish registers in this library. A *Handlist of Church of Ireland parish registers in the Representative Church Body Library* (which is updated regularly) is available from the library by post for a fee.

The Presbyterian Historical Society Library
This is located at Church House (Room 218), Fisherwick Place, Belfast, BT1 6DW. Tel: +44 (0)28 90 323936.
Open: 10 am to 12.30 pm Monday to Friday and also on Wednesday from 2 pm to 4 pm.
This Library contains manuscript material concerning Presbyterian families. It has baptismal and marriage records of Presbyterian Churches in Ireland, many of these are on microfilm here and in the Public Records Office Belfast, The Library has three card indexes: one is for published sources, the second is for manuscript sources and the third is for church registers. There is a file of family records in the form of brief biographical and genealogical notes compiled in the course of various searches. Among the sources in the Library are: The Heartmoney Rolls 1663-69 for the counties of Antrim, part of Armagh, Derry, Tyrone and the Subsidy Roll of County Down; the 1774 Householder's list; the 1766 Religious Census; the 1775 Petitions of Dissenters. The index to the church registers 367 congregations throughout Ireland.

Religious Society of Friends Historical Library
The Friends (Quakers) Library is located at Swanbrook House, Morehampton Road, Donnybrook, Dublin 4.
Tel: (01): 6683684, 6687157.
It is open 10.30 am to 1 pm on Thursdays, to arrange access at other times one should telephone.
The Irish Manuscripts Commission has published a *Guide to Irish Quaker Records* (1967), Part II of which lists documents available in this library.
There is also a library located at: Friends Meeting House, Railway Street, Lisburn, Co Antrim, which library has records dating from 1673.

Irish Jewish Museum
The Irish Jewish Museum is located at 3/4 Walworth Road, South Circular Road, Dublin 8. This Museum contains registers of births, marriages and deaths. It is open from 11 am to 3.30 pm, Monday, Wednesday and Sunday from May to September and from 10.30 am to 2.30 pm on Sundays from October to April.

Dublin Local Studies Collection / The Gilbert Library
This Library (which is part of the Dublin Public Libraries) is located above Pearce Street Public Library, Pearce Street, Dublin.
Tel: +353 (01) 677 7662.
NOTE closed for renovation reopening 2003.
www.ireland.iol.ie/resourse/dublincitylibrary/gasources.htm
It is open Monday to Friday (10 am to 1 pm, 2.15pm to 5.30, closing at 5 pm on Friday), and Saturday (10 am to 1 pm, 1.45 pm to 4.30 pm).
Amongst the sources for family history here are:
Griffith's Valuation - microfiche
Tithe Applotment Books - microfilm
Ordnance Survey first edition 6-inch maps -
Ordnance Survey Letters of John O'Donovan
Census Returns 1901 for Dublin - microfilm
Church of Ireland Parish Registers for Dublin - microfilm
The Famine Immigrants 1846-1851
Memorial Records (The Great War)
Index to wills.

Belfast Central Library
This public library is on Royal Avenue, in Belfast BT1 IEA.
It opens at 9.30 pm Monday to Saturday, closing at 8 pm Monday and Thursday; 5.30 pm Tuesday, Wednesday and Friday; and at 1 pm on Saturday.

The Irish and Local Studies Library on the first floor has a stock of over 50,000 books, maps, photographs and manuscripts containing material about Irish life with particular reference to Belfast.

Centre for Migration Studies
This is located at the Ulster American Folk Park, Castletown, Omagh, Tyrone, BT78 5 QY. Tel: +44 (0)28 82 243292, *www.folkpark.com*.
The Research Library comprises a specialist collection of printed materials and an Emigration Database. This database is a computerized collection of primary sources on Irish emigration to North America. It includes emigrant letters, newspaper articles, shipping advertisements, passenger lists, official government reports, family papers and extracts from books and periodicals. The Database can also be accessed in the Local Studies Departments of libraries in Armagh, Ballymena, Ballynahinch, Belfast, Derry, Enniskillen, and Omagh.

Family Record Centre
This is located at Myddelton Street, Islington, London EC1R 1UW.
www.familyrecords.gov.uk/frc.htm
It opens 9 am to 5 pm Monday, Wednesday and Friday; 10 am to 7 pm Tuesday; 9 am to 7 pm Thursday; and 9.30 am to 5 pm Saturday.
The General Registers Office, which is part of the Office of National Statistics, has its search room on the ground floor of this building. The civil registers of births, marriage and death from 1st July 1837 for England and Wales are here. Tel: +44 (0)870 243 7788.
The Public Records Office occupies the first floor of this building and microfilm copies of many of its genealogical records are here. These include: Census Returns 1841-1901; Death Duty Registers 1796-1858; Wills and Administrations (Canterbury) 1383-1858; and Nonparochal registers 1567-1858.
www.englishorigins.com in association with the Society of Genealogists has an online search facility, costing £6 for 150 credits for 48 consecutive hours.

Public Records Office
This is located at Ruskin Avenue, Kew, Surrey TW9 4DU.
Tel: +44 (0)20 8876 3444; Fax: 8393 5286
Search rooms are open 9.30 am to 5 pm Monday to Friday.
A reader's ticket will be issued on production of identification.
This is the British national archive with particular reference to England and Wales. However records relating to Ireland, Scotland and the former British Empire are here. It houses records of the central government and

law courts from the Doomsday Book in 1086 to the present. There are a great number of genealogical records here, to which reference has been made elsewhere. This office has a publication: *Tracing Your Ancestors in the Public Records Office*, which is worth consulting.

National Archives of Scotland

This is the new name for the Scottish Records Office located at General Register House, Edinburgh, EH1 3YY. This building is also known as "Old Register House". *www.nas.gov.uk/*

The Search Rooms are open: 9 am to 4.45 pm Monday to Friday.

Reader's tickets are issued on personal application. Records are made available without charge for historical research.

Amongst the materials of genealogical interest are:

Wills and Testaments. From the sixteenth century to the present.

Sasines and other property records. These are records of transactions in land. All are indexed and some are available in print.

Estate records. For ancestors who were tenants on landed estates.

Valuation Rolls 1855-1975. List proprietors, tenants and occupiers.

Taxation Records. Hearth and poll tax records compiled in the 1690s and eighteenth century taxation lists.

Court Records. Both civil and criminal.

Church Records. Records of different denominations with various information.

Burgh Records. Includes list of inhabitants, apprenticeship and burgess rolls, and craft and guildry records.

General Register Office for Scotland

This is located at New Register House, Edinburgh EH1 3YT. *www.gro-scotland.gov.uk/*. Records may be searched online at *www.scotsorigins.com/*. Access costs £6 for 30 page credit valid for 24 consecutive hours. There is a free surname search.

It is open from 9 am to 4.30 pm Monday to Friday.

The records here include:

Old parish registers (1553 to 1854). Approximately 3,500 registers have survived from the period prior to the introduction of compulsory civil registration in 1855.

Register of neglected entries (1801 to 1854). This is a register of births, marriages and deaths, which had not been entered in the parish registers.

Registers of births, deaths and marriages from 1st January 1855. Consultation is from microfiche.

Census records from 1841. The records are transcript books prepared by the census enumerators and contain name, age, marital status, occupation, and birthplace.

In order to conduct a general search the public must pay. There are a limited number of places available, but advance booking is possible. Members of staff will make a particular search upon payment.

The National Library of Wales
This library is in Aberystwyth, Ceredigion, SY23 3BU, Wales. *www.llgc.org.uk/ht/index_s.htm*. There is a search service.
The reading rooms are open:
9.30 pm to 6 pm on weekdays; and
9.30 pm to 5 pm on Saturday.
Both long and short term readers' tickets may be issued. Short term ticket are normally issued for one day but may be extended for six days. Long term tickets are issued for five years and are renewable.
Amongst the materials of genealogical interest are:
Indexes of Births, Marriages and Deaths 1837-1983. Microfiche copies may be searched free of charge.
Census Returns 1841-1891. Microform copies of the returns for the whole of Wales for each of the ten-yearly censuses. In addition there are indexes available for some returns.
International Genealogical Index (IGI) for the British Isles is available on microfiche.
Parish Registers. Registers of nearly 500 parishes together with copies of others.
Diocesan Records of the Anglican Church. These include: Bishops' Transcripts; Marriage Bonds and Affidavits; Ordination Papers; Clergy Visitation Books; and Consistory Court Papers.
NonConformist Records. Microfilm copies of pre-1837 registers for Wales which are in the British Public Records Office, in addition there are some actual registers.
Wills and Administrations. Wills proved in the Welsh Ecclesiastical Courts from 1543-1858. In addition the Calendar of State Grants from 1858 to 1972.
Together with in brief: Great Session Records; Quarter Session Records; Poor Law Records; Education Records;
Manorial Records; Estate Records and personal Papers; and Pedigree Books.

The Family History Library
This is located at 35 North West Temple, Salt Lake City, Utah (UT 84150-3400), United States. Tel: +1 801 240 2331 or 800 453 3860 x22321; Fax: 801 240 1584.   E-mail fhl@ldschurch.org.

ww.familysearch.org/Eng/library/FHL/frameset_library.asp.

The library has the largest collection of genealogical records on Earth. It was established in 1894 by the Church of Jesus Christ of Latter-day Saints to collect genealogical records and to help Church members trace their ancestors. It is open to the public without charge, visited by an estimated 2000 each day.

It is safe to assume that most records already referred to are here. There are more than 11,500 microfilms, 3,000 microfiche, and 3,500 books, periodicals and other printed materials on Ireland. The library has three major collections of previous research that has been already done by others:

Family group records collection

This consists of millions of forms with information on families all over the World. The information has been submitted by users of the library and has not been verified.

International Genealogical Index (IGI)

This is an index of the names of persons with details of baptisms and marriage, it is compiled predominantly from parish registers and is a convenient way to prepare for searching parish registers. This database contains approximately 600 million names, and an addendum contains an additional 125 million names. There are 1.4 million names of those who lived in Ireland.

Family histories

The library has thousand of family histories. Some of these are books and some are microfilm or microfiche copies.

The records for the British Isles are on the third floor and the staff are both helpful and professional. A visit to this library by a genealogist is well worth the trek to Utah.

There are Family History Centres throughout the world, which are branches of the library. Most are located in meetinghouses of churches and all persons irrespective of religious affiliation are welcome to use the centres. Volunteers will help you use the resources at each centre. A person can do a great deal of genealogical research at these centres by requesting copies of records from the Family History Library. Most records are on microfilm or microfiche and can be loaned to a centre for a reasonable fee. The centres are not able to respond to postal inquiries.

LDS Family History Centre Dublin

This is located at the rear of the Church of Jesus Christ of The Latter Day Saints at Finglas Road, Glasnevin, Dublin 11. Tel: (01) 8309960.

Open: Tuesday, Wednesday, Thursday, Friday 7 pm to 9 pm. Thursday 12.30 pm to 4.30 pm.

This Library has on microfilm the indices for births, marriage and death from 1845/1864 to 1921 for the whole of Ireland and to 1959 for the twenty-six counties. In addition it has on microfilm actual registers for the 1800's and the I.G.I. on microfiche.

LDS Family History Centre Belfast
This is located at the rear of the Church of Jesus Christ of The Latter Day Saints at 403 Holywood Road, Belfast.
Tel: + 44 (0)28 90 76 8250 / 64 3998.
Open: Wednesday/Thursday 10 am to 4 pm; Saturday 9 am to 1 pm.
This library has on microfiche: The Genealogical Library Catalogue, which lists the complete holdings of the Family Library in Salt Lake City. The International Genealogical Index referred to above. The indices for births, marriage and death from 1845/1864 to 1921 for the whole of Ireland and to 1959 for the six counties. In addition the cenre has on microfilm the actual registers for births and deaths to 1877 and for marriages to 1870. A few reference books and guides are also available for consultation.

Cork
Scarsfield Road, Wilton, Cork. Tel: 00 353 (0)1 341 737.
Open: Tuesday 10 am to 12 pm and Wednesday 7 pm to 9 pm.

Limerick
Doradoyle Road, Limerick. Open: Friday 7 pm to 9 pm.

Colraine
8 Sandelfield, Colraine, Derry. +44 (0)28 90 321214.
Open: Tuesday 9.30 am to 2.30 pm; Wednesday 6.30 pm to 8.30 pm.

Derry
Racecourse Road, Belmont Estate, Derry. NOTE closed for renovation.

National Archives of the United States
This is located at Pennsylvania Avenue at 8th Street, NW Washington DC 20408. *www.archives.gov/research_room/genealogy/index.html*
Tel +1 86 NARA NARA; 866 272 6272.
There are Field branches in Atlanta; Boston; Chicago; Denver; Forth Worth; Kansas City, Los Angeles; New York; Philadelphia; San Francisco; and Seattle.
There is a vast collection of federal documents, which include census; land; immigration records; and military records. The federal government every ten years since 1790 has taken censuses. Note that state and local government also took censuses. Passenger arrival records can help determine when an ancestor arrived and the port of departure. Military records from 1789 to present some of which have been microfilmed. A *Guide to Genealogical Research in the National Archives* (Third Edition 2001) $39/$25, should be consulted.

American Family Immigration History Center

This is located in the Ellis Island Immigration Museum, New York City. It is also at *www.ellisisland.org*. More than 22 million passengers entered the United States through Ellis Island between 1892 and 1924. The Passenger Record Archive may be searched in person (search sessions cost $5) or online.

National Archives of Canada

The headquarters building is located at 395 Wellington Street, Ottawa, Ontario K1A ON3. *www.archives.ca*
Tel: toll free (Canada/USA) 1 866 578 7777; Genealogy reference 613 996 7458; Fax: 613 995 6274. There is both a mail and electronic inquiry service.
The reading room is open: 8.30 am to 10 pm Monday to Friday, and 8 am to 6 pm Saturday and Sunday.
Amongst the genealogical sources available are: Census records; Birth, marriage death, divorce and adoption records, Land records; Wills and estate records; Military records; Immigration records; Citizenship records; School records; and Newspapers. There is a free publication available online *Tracing your Ancestors in Canada*.
There is a decentralized access site at: University of Saskatchewan Archives, 301 Murray Building (Main Library), 3 Campus Drive, University of Saskatchewan, Saskatoon, SK S7N OWO. Tel: +1 306 966 6028; Fax: 306 966 6040; E-mail *university.archives@usask.ca*

National Archives of Australia

Is located in Canberra, P.O. Box 7425, Canberra Mail Centre, Australian Capital Territory 2610. *www.naa.gov.au/*
There are regional offices in each state. Amongst the records of genealogical interest are: business; immigration; military; and naturalization. A guide is *Relations in records: a Guide to Family History Sources in the Australian Archives*.
The National Library of Australia, Parkes Place, Canberra, ACT 2600, has genealogical materials.
Archive Office of New South Wales, 2 Globe Street, The Rocks, Sydney, New South Wales 2000.
South Australia State Archives, P.O. Box 123, Rundle Mall, Adelaide, South Australia 5001. Publication: *Ancestors in Archives: a guide to family history sources in the official records of South Australia*.
Archives Office of Tasmania, 77 Murray Street, Hobart, Tasmania 7000.
Public Records Office, Level 19 Nauru House, 80 Collins Street, Melbourne, Victoria 3000.
Western Australia State Archives, Alexander Library Building, Perth Cultural Centre, Perth, Western Australia.

Records at the State Archives include: birth, marriage, and death records, court, directories, electoral rolls, land, and shipping.
In addition there are State Libraries.

Archives New Zealand
The head office is located at 10 Mulgrave Street, Thorndon, Wellington.
P.O. Box 12-050 Wellington, New Zealand. *www.archives.govt.nz*
Tel: (64-4) 499 5595; Helpdesk (64-4) 495 6226; Fax: 495 6210.
E-mail: Wellington@archives.govt.nz.
Open: Monday to Friday 9 am – 5 pm; Saturday (Exhibitions) 9 am-1 pm.
Amongst the genealogical records included are:
Records of government assisted immigrants from 1840 to 1888, and ships' passenger lists from the 1880s to 1972.
Probate files on the administration of deceased estates, and usually include a copy of the deceased's will.
Notices of intention to marry contain additional information to the marriage certificate. They cover the period from 1856 to 1956.
Military service records prior to 1913.
National Library www.natlib.govt.nz/en/
This is situated in Wellington, on the corner of Aitken and Molesworth Street. The Family History Collection is open Monday to Friday 9 am-5 pm: and on Saturday 9 am to 1 pm. The Alexander Turnbull Collection includes newspapers, and the index to civil registration to 1990 is here.
Births, Deaths and Marriages Registry
Copies of Birth and Death Records from 1848 and Marriage Records from 1854 are available.
Auckland City Library has Family History Databases. The Auckland Area Passenger Arrivals cover the period 1838 to 1883.
www.aucklandcitylibraries.com
The New Zealand Society of Genealogists has an Irish Interest Group.
www.genealogy.org.nz

National Archives of South Africa
The head office is located at 24 Hamilton Street, Arcadia, Pretoria.
www.national.archives.gov.za
The postal address is Private Bag X236, Pretoria 0001. Tel: (012) 323 5300; Fax: 323 5287. E-mail arg02@dacst4.pwv.gov.za.
There are Archives Repositories in Cape Town and Bloemfontein, in addition there are separate provincial repositories.
The registration of births, marriages, and death is the responsibility of the Department of Home Affairs.

Chapter 14

Distribution of Surnames

The principal surnames for each county is listed, they are in order of the numerical strength in which they occur. The figure after the surname is the number of entries in the birth index for 1890. The estimated number of persons of each surname can be ascertained by multiplying the figure by the average birth rate, which for that year was 1 in 44.8 persons. This material is taken from Matheson's work.

Although 'Murphy' is the most numerous surname in the country at large, it does not occupy the leading position in many of the counties. In Leinster in the counties of Wexford and Carlow 'Murphy' is first. In the counties of: Dublin; Louth; and Wicklow. 'Byrne' is first, whereas in Kildare and Offaly 'Kelly' is first. In Longford and Meath, 'Reilly' is first, in Kilkenny, Brennan, in Laois 'Dunne', and in Westmeath 'Lynch'. In Munster, 'Sullivan' is the predominant surname in Cork and Kerry, followed in Cork by 'Murphy'. 'Ryan' heads the list in Limerick and Tipperary, while 'McMahon' is the leading surname in Clare, and 'Power' in Waterford. In Ulster 'Murphy' is the first surname in Armagh only. In Antrim 'Smith' is first, in Cavan, 'Reilly', in Donegal, 'Gallagher', in Down 'Thompson', in Fermanagh 'Maguire', in Derry, 'Doherty', in Monaghan, 'Duffey', and in Tyrone 'Quinn'. In Connaught, 'Kelly' takes precedence in Galway, Roscommon, and Leitrim (along with Reynolds), Murphy does not occupy the principal position in any county. Walsh is first in Mayo, and Brennan in Sligo.

Province of Leinster

Carlow
Murphy 41, Byrne 33, Doyle 32, Nolan 28, Neill 27, Brennan 24, Kelly 15, McDonald 15, Kavanagh 14, Whelan 12, Ryan 10.

Dublin
Byrne 301, Kelly 194, Doyle 162, Murphy 132, Smith 106, O'Brien 105, Kavanagh 97, Dunne 93, O'Neill 93, Reilly 93, Nolan 89, Connor 82, Walsh 77, Farrell 73, Carroll 71, Ryan 65, Moore 63, Cullen 62, Keogh 60, Murray 60, Whelan 59, Brady 52, Kennedy 51.

Kildare
Kelly 40, Murphy 34, Dunne 32, Byrne 28, Nolan 20, Connor 18, Smith

65

18, Farrell 15, Ryan 15, Moore 14, Carroll 13, O'Neill 13, Bolger 12, Doyle 12.

Kilkenny

Brennan 49, Walsh 45, Murphy 35, Ryan 34, Carroll 25, Byrne 22, Butler 22, Maher 21, Dunne 20, Phelan 18, Kelly 17, Neill 17, Power 17, Purcell 17, Brien 15, Shea 15, Delaney, 14, Dowling 14.

Laois (Queen's)

Dunne 34, Delaney 30, Conroy 19, Lalor 18, Phelan 18, Fitzpatrick 17, Ryan 13, Carroll 12, Whelan 12, Byrne 11, Kavanagh 11, Kennedy 11, Brennan 10, Kelly 10, Murphy 10.

Longford

Reilly 78, Farrell 36, Kiernan 24, Kelly 23, Donohoe 19, Murphy 14, Brady 13, Quinn 12, Smith 12.

Louth

Byrne 36, Kelly 30, Murphy 30, Smith 26, Clarke 23, Duffy 21, McArdle 20, Reilly 20, Carroll 19, Mathews 16, Martin 14, Donnelly 13, Farrell 13, Morgan 13, Rice 13, Hanratty 12, McCourt 12, McKenna 12, Boyle 11, Connor 11, Lynch 11, O'Hare 11.

Offaly (King's)

Kelly 34, Dunne 23, Daly 20, Egan 17, Molloy 16, Mooney 16, Carroll 12, Walsh 12, Kenny 11, Murray 11, Dempsey 10, Kennedy 10, Maher 10.

Meath

Reilly 53, Smith 30, Lynch 17, Brady 16, Farrell 14, Farrelly 14, Kelly 14, Brien 13, Daly 11, Maguire 11, Duffy 9, Dunne 9, Byrne 8, Connor 8, Mahon 7, Clarke 7, Martin 7, Mathews 7.

Westmeath

Lynch 14, Farrell 13, Reilly 12, Daly 11, Murray 10, Duffy 9, McCormick 9, Walsh 9, Dalton 8, Kelly 8, Smith 8, Byrne 7, Carey 7, Dunne 6, Flynn 6, Leavy 6, Murtagh 6, O'Neill 6.

Wexford

Murphy 137, Doyle 102, Walsh 56, Byrne 46, Cullen 34, Kavanagh 34, Brien 32, Roche 31, Kelly 30, Nolan 30, Redmond 30, Connor 28, Kehoe 28, Ryan 26, Bolger 25, Whelan 25.

Wicklow
Byrne 87, Doyle 53, Murphy 26, Kelly 25, Kavanagh 24, Nolan 21, Brien 18, Kehoe 16, Lawlor 15, Toole 14, Dunne 13, Farrell 11, Redmond 10.

Province of Munster

Clare
McMahon 74, McNamara 61, Moloney 50, O'Brien 47, McInerney 39, Kelly 38, Keane 33, Murphy 29, Griffin 27, Halloran 26, Ryan 23, Lynch 22, Clancey 21.

Cork
Sullivan 418, Murphy 390, McCarthy 277, Mahoney 193, Donovan 182, Walsh 143, O'Brien 139, Callaghan 134, Leary 134, Crowley 116, Collins 115, Driscoll 110, Connell 109, Barry 108, Cronin 102, Buckley 100, Daly 97, Sheehan 97, Riordan 94, Kelleher 92, O'Connor 91, Hurley 86, Regan 85, O'Keeffe 84, Harrington 82, Fitzgerald 81, O'Neill 75.

Kerry
Sullivan 349, Connor 188, Shea 146, Murphy 95, McCarthy 88, Moriarty 74, Fitzgerald 72, Griffin 58, Connell 56, Brosnan 55, Foley 55, Leary 47, Clifford 45, Walsh 45, Cronin 43, Lynch 41, Mahoney 38, Daly 34.

Limerick
Ryan 91, O'Brien 78, Fitzgerald 58, Sullivan 50, Hayes 45, Walsh 45, Collins 40, O'Connell 39, Murphy 38, Moloney 38, O'Connor 37, Lynch 31, McNamara 31, O'Donnell 28, Ahern 25.

Tipperary
Ryan 277, Maher 74, O'Brien 74, Kennedy 70, Dwyer 64, Hogan 46, Hayes 38, Gleeson 38, Mc Grath 38, Walsh 38, Kelly 31, Lonergan 31.

Waterford
Power 125, Walsh 97, O'Brien 47, Murphy 35, Ryan 35, McGrath 31, Foley 30, Flynn 28, Morrissey 27, Kelly 26, Phelan 25, Sullivan 25, Whelan 23, McCarthy 22, Butler 21, Tobin 20.

Province of Ulster

Antrim
Smith 134, Johnston 126, Stewart 126, Wilson 119, Thompson 101, O'Neill 98, Campbell 96, Moore 96, Bell 90, Robinson 89, Millar 86,

Brown 82, Boyd 81, Scott 66, Graham 64, Reid 63, Martin 61, Kerr 60, Hamilton 50.

Armagh
Murphy 50, Hughes 47, Wilson 45, Campbell 42, O'Hare 37, Smith 31, McCann 29, Donnelly 28, Watson 28, Quinn 26, Johnston 25, Kelly 25, Thompson 23.

Cavan
Reilly 137, Smith 108, Brady 85, Lynch 51, McCabe 36, Clarke 30, Farrelly 29, Maguire 26, Sheridan 26, Galligan 20, Fitzpatrick 19, Dolan 18, McGovern 18, Donohoe 17, Martin 15, McMahon 15.

Derry (Londonderry)
Doherty 80, McLaughlin 68, Kelly 50, Bradley 40, Brown 36, McCloskey 36, Campbell 33, Mullan 33, Smith 31, O'Neill 29, Kane 26, Moore 25, Gallagher 23.

Donegal
Gallagher 196, Doherty 160, Boyle 102, O'Donnell 102, McLaughlin 81, Sweeney 50, Ward 40, Kelly 37, McGinley 37, McFadden 33, McGowan 33, Duffy 33, Campbell 28.

Down
Thompson 55, Smith 53, Campbell 45, Patterson 41, Martin 35, Wilson 35, Graham 34, Johnston 34, Murray 33, Brown 31, Robinson 29, Hamilton 28, Bell 27, Scott 27, Boyd 25.

Fermanagh
Maguire 44, McManus 30, Dolan 23, McGovern 23, Johnston 22, McHugh 20, Cassidy 17, Wilson 15, Thompson 14, Elliott 13, Irvine 13, McLoughlin 12, Gallagher 11, Murphy 11, Reilly 11, Fitzpatrick 10, Flanagan 10.

Monaghan
Duffy 38, Connolly 36, McMahon 33, McKenna 32, Hughes 25, Murphy 24, McCabe 22, Martin 19, Smith 19, Keily 18, Quinn 18, Maguire 17, Murphy 17, Woods 14.

Tyrone
Quinn 40, Mullan 39, Kelly 38, Donnelly 34, Gallagher 34, McKenna 33, Campbell 32, Hughes 31, Wilson 30, McLaughlin 29, O'Neill 29, Doherty 27, Smith 25, Hamilton 23.

Province of Connaught

Galway
Kelly 119, Burke 89, Conneely 89, Joyce 85, McDonagh 80, Walsh 80, Fahy 63, Mannion 59, Flaherty 48, Murphy 47, Connolly 46, Keane 40, King 36, Forde 35, Connor 33, Lyons 30, Mullin 30, Egan 29, Kenny 27, Toole 25.

Leitrim
Kelly 30, Reynolds 30, Flynn 20, McLoughlin 20, McHugh 19, Rooney 18, McMorrow 18, McTernan 17, Keany 16, McGowan 16, Moran 16, Reilly 16, Maguire 15, Dolan 14, Beirne 13, Gallagher 13, McDermott 13, McGovern 13, McSharry 13, Mulvey 13.

Mayo
Walsh 134, Gallagher 92, Kelly 89, Malley 78, Moran 77, Duffy 55, McHale 50, Gibbons 47, Joyce 46, Connor 45, Conway 40, Higgins 39, Murphy 39, Burke 36, Reilly 36, Durkan 35, Doherty 34, McHugh 34, Sweeney 33, Lyons 32.

Roscommon
Kelly 68, McDermott 45, Beirne 38, Regan 35, Flanagan 32, Connor 30, McDonagh 26, Quinn 25, Murray 24, Brennan 22, Higgins 22, Towey 22, Kenny 21, Flynn 20.

Sligo
Brennan 31, McLoughlin 28, Gallagher 26, Kelly 23, Harte 20, McGowan 18, Walsh 18, Kennedy 16, Durkan 15, Henry 15, Flynn 14, Gilmartin 14, Leonard 14, Scanlon 14, Connolly 13, O'Hara 13, Feeney 11, Stenson 11, Conway 10, Sheridan 10.

Chapter 15

Hundred most numerous surnames

What follows is a note on the hundred most numerous surnames in order of numerical strength. The information given in respect of each surname is; anglicised form, Irish form, meaning of the root word upon which the surname was based, the estimated number of persons bearing the name in 1890, which information is taken from the *Special Report on Surnames* by Matheson. The estimated population of Ireland in 1890 was 4,717,959 persons.

There are many English and Scottish names. Additional information provided is the place the name occupies in the most numerous list for England and Wales (EW.), and for Scotland (S.).

1   **Murphy** ó Murchadha, Mac Murchaidh, ó Murchú, *sea-battler,* 62,600.
2   **(O')Kelly** ó Ceallaigh, *bright-headed,* 55,900.
3   **(O')Sullivan** ó Súilleabháin, *dark-eyed,* 43,600
4   **Walsh** Breathnach, *Welshman,* 41,700
5   **Smith, MacGowan** Mac Gabhann, *son of the smith,* 33,700 EW. 1, S. 1.
6   **O'Brien** ó Briain, *high, noble,* 33,400
7   **Byrne** ó Broin, *a raven,* 33,300
8   **Ryan** ó Maoilriain, ó Riain, *King,* 32,000,
9   **O'Connor** ó Conchobhair, *patron of warriors,* 31,200
10   **O'Neill** ó Néill, *from Niall Naoi nGiallach,* 29,100
11   **O'Reilly** ó Raghallaigh, 29,000
12   **Doyle** ó Dubhghaill, ó Dúill, *black foreigner,* 23,000
13   **McCarthy** Mac Carthaigh, *loving person,* 22,300
14   **Gallagher** ó Gallchobhair, ó Gallchóir, *lover of foreigners*, 21,800,
15   **O'Doherty** ó Dochartaigh, *hurtful,* 20,800
16   **(O')Kennedy** ó Cinnéide, *rough-headed, helmeted-head*, 19,900.
17   **Lynch** ó Loingsigh, *seafarer, exile,* 19,800
18   **Murray** ó Muireadhaigh, ó Muirí, *lord, master,* 19,600, S. 17.
19   **Quinn** ó Cuinn, *wisdom, chief,* 18,200
20   **Moore** ó Mórdha, ó Móra, *majestic,* 17,700, EW. 39.
21   **McLaughlin** Mac Lochlainn, *Viking,* 17,500
22   **(O')Carroll** ó Cearbhaill, ó Cearúill, *valorous in battle,* 17,500
23   **Connolly** ó Conghaile, *fierce as a hound,* 17,000
24   **Daly** ó Dálaigh, *given to frequenting assemblies,* 17,000
25   **O'Connell** ó Chonaill, ó Conaill, *strong as a wolf,* 16,600

26 **Wilson** Mac Liam, *son of William,* 16,300, S. 8, EW. 11.

27 **Dunne** ó Duinn, ó Doinn, *brown,* 16,300

28 **Brennan** ó Braonáin, *sorrow,* 16,000

29 **Burke** de Búrca, *descendants of Richard de Burgh,* 15,900

30 **Collins** ó Coileáin, Mac Coileáin, *young warrior,* 15,700

31 **Campbell, Mac Cathmhaoil,** *crooked mouth,* 15,600, S. 7

32 **Clarke** ó Cléirigh, *cleric, clergyman,* 15,400, S. 18, EW. 41.

33 **Johns(t)on(e)** Mac Iain, Mac Seáin, *son of John,* 15,200, EW. 10, S. 16.

34 **Hughes** ó hAodha, *fire,* 14,900, EW. 19.

35 **(O')Farrell** ó Fearghail, ó Fearail, *man of valour,* 14,700

36 **Fitzgerald** Mac Gearailt, OG *spear rule,* 14,700

37 **Brown** de Brún, Mac an Bhreithiún, *son of the brehon (Judge)* 14,600, S. 3, EW. 6.

38 **Martin, MacGillmartin,** ó Máirtín, Mac Giolla Mháirtín, *devotee of Saint Martin,* 14,600, EW. 31, S. 48.

39 **Maguire** Mag Uidhir, *dun-coloured,* 14,400

40 **Nolan, Knowlan** ó Nualláin, *famous,* 14,300

41 **(O')Flynn** ó Floinn, *bright red, blood red,* 14,300

42 **Thom(p)son** Mac Thómais, *son of Thom,* 14,200, S. 4, EW.15.

43 **(O')Callaghan** ó Ceallacháin, *bright-headed,* 14,000

44 **O'Donnell** ó Domhnaill, ó Donaill, *world mighty,* 13,900

45 **(O')Duffy** ó Dubhthaigh, ó Dufaigh, *dark, black,* 13,600

46 **(O')Mahoney** ó Mathghamhna, ó Mathúna, *bear-calf,* 13,500

47 **(O')Boyle** ó Baoighhil, ó Baoill, *vain pledge,* 13,000

48 **Healy** ó hEalaighthe, ó hEalaithe, ó hEilí, *artistic, scientific,* 13,000.

49 **(O')Shea** ó Séaghdha, ó Sé, *fine, stately* 13,000

50 **White** Mac Giolla Bháin, de Faoite, *of fair complexion,* 13,000, EW. 22, S. 41.

51 **(Mc)Sweeney** Mac Suibhne, *pleasant,* 12,500

52 **Hayes** ó hAodha, *fire,* 12,300

53 **Kavanagh** Caomhánach, *comely, mild,* 12,200

54 **Power** de Paor, *the poor man,* 12,100

55 **McGrath** Mac Craith, *son of grace,* 11,900

56 **Moran** ó Móráin, *great,* 11,800

57 **Brady** Mac Brádaigh, Bradach *spirited,* 11,600

58 **Stewart, Stuart,** Stiobhard, *one who superintends,* 11,400, S. 6.

59 **Casey** ó Cathasaigh, Cathasach, *vigilant in war, watchful* 11,300

60 **Foley** ó Foghladha, ó Foghlú, *plunderer,* 11,200

61 **Fitzpatrick** MacGiolla Phádraig, *devotee St Patrick,* 11,100

62 **(O')Leary** ó Laoghaire, ó Laoire, *calf-herd,* 11,000

63 **MacDonnell** Mac Domhnaill, *world-mighty,* 11,000

64 **MacMahon** Mac Mathghamhna, Mac Mathúna, *bear-calf,* 10,700
65 **Donnelly** ó Donnghaile, ó Donnaile, *brown-valour,* 10,700
66 **(O')Regan** ó Riagáin, ó Réagáin, *little king* 10,500
67 **(O')Donovan** ó Donnabháin, *brown, black,* 9,900
68 **Burns** Burness, *local origin, Scotland,* 9,800
69 **Flanagan** ó Flannagáin, *red or ruddy,* 9,800
70 **Mullan** ó Maoláin, *bald,* 9,800
71 **Barry** de Barra, *N local origin,* 9,700
72 **(O')Kane** ó Catháin, *battler,* 9,700
73 **Robinson** *son of Robert,* 9,700, S. 5, EW. 12.
74 **Cunningham,** Mac Cuinneagáin, from *Conn,* also local origin in Scotland, 9,600
75 **Griffin** ó Gríobhtha, ó Gríofa, gríhtha, *OW Gruffudd,* 9,600
76 **Kenny** ó Cionaoith, *fire-sprung,* 9,600
77 **Sheehan** ó Síodhacháin, ó Síocháin *peaceful,* 9,600
78 **Ward** Mac an Bháird, *son of the bard,* 9,500, EW. 30.
79 **Whelan** ó Faoláin, *wolf,* 9,500
80 **Lyons** ó Laighin, ó Liatháin, *Leinsterman, grey*, 9,400
81 **Reid** *red haired, ruddy complexion,* 9,200, S. 13.
82 **Graham** *grey home, S.,* 9,100, S. 40.
83 **Higgins** ó hUiginn, 9,100
84 **Cullen** ó Cuilinn, *holly,* 9,000
85 **Keane** Mac Cahan(e), Mac Catháin, 9,000
86 **King** ó Cionga, 9,000, EW. 36.
87 **Maher** Meagher, ó Meachai, *fine, majestic*, 9,000
88 **MacKenna** Mac Cionaoith, *fire-sprung* 9,000
89 **Bell** Mac Giolla Mhaoil, 8,800, S. 47.
90 **Scott** *A Scottish Gael,* 8,700, S. 10.
91 **Hogan** ó hOgáin, *young,* 8,600
92 **O'Keeffe** ó Caoimh, *gentle,* 8,600
93 **Magee** Mag Aoidh, *fire* 8,600
94 **MacNamara** Mac Conmara, *hound of the sea,* 8,600
95 **MacDonald** Mac Dónaill, *world mighty,* 8,500, S. 2.
96 **MacDermot(t)** Mac Diarmada, *free from jealousy,* 8,400
97 **Moloney** ó Maolomhnaigh, *servant of the Church,* 8,300
98 **(O')Rourke** ó Ruairc, 8,300
99 **Buckley** ó Buachalla, *cow herd,* 8,200
100 **O'Dwyer** ó Duibhir, ó Dubhuir, *black,* 8,100

Chapter 16

Keeping family records

Having accumulated genealogical information, what is the best method of keeping such information? Family records may be kept on paper or on computer.

With respect to paper records pedigree charts and family record sheets are to be recommended (See following Pages). Copies of such paper forms (and many others) can be downloaded from the Internet. There are many sources for such forms: *www.FamilyTreeMagazine.com* - which includes a research log; research worksheet; note taking forms; military checklist; and U.S. census forms,
www.cs.williams.edu/-bailey/genealogy/,
www.pbs.org/kbvu/ancestors/charts/ - PDF files include pedigree chart; family group sheet; research questions; research logs; and source notes,
www.enoch.com/genealogy/forms.htm - pedigree chart; family group sheet; research log; and U.S. census form.

There are many computer genealogy programmes now available. Two well known such programmes are available free to download over the Internet. Personal Ancestral File (PAF) from the LDS, www.familysearch.org, and Legacy Family Tree 3.0, from www.legacyfamilytree.com. In addition other programmes may be downloaded on a trial basis. The appropriate links will also be found via *www.IrishAncestors.net*.

Using pedigree charts

Pedigree charts are used as follows, if you decide that you are going to chart your own ancestry then you are number 1. You list your father as 2, and your mother as 3, your paternal grandfather's paternal grandfather as 16, your paternal grandmother's paternal grandfather as 20, your maternal grandfather's paternal grandfather as 24, and your maternal grandmother's paternal grandfather as 28. If you decide that your children are number 1, then if male, you are 2, and your spouse 3. If you are female, you are 3, and your spouse is 2.

Abbreviations used in charts are as follows:

b	date of birth	**w**	where born
m	date of marriage	**w**	where married
d	date of death	**w**	where died

Example of Chart use (My own children being number **1**):

                                              8. John Quinn

                         4. Daniel Joseph Quinn

                                          9. Ann Jane Murray

    2. Seán Eoghan Quinn

                                       10. Con McLaughlin

                         5. Ena McLaughlin

                                     11. Hannah Barr

1. Ena Kathleen
1. Niall Domhnall Mel
1. Eoghan Conall Mel

                                     12. Edward Farrell

                         6. Edward Farrell

                                     13. Margaret Scally

    3. Anne Farrell

                                     14. Patrick Brennan

                         7. Kathleen Brennan

                                     15. Mary Ann Hopkins

Family Record Sheet

Husband_____
b/w_____
m/w_____
d/w_____
Father_____ Mother_____
_____

Wife_____
b/w_____
m/w_____
d/w_____
Father_____ Mother_____
_____

Children	Born	Where	Married

1._____
2._____
3._____
4._____
5._____
6._____
7._____
8._____
9._____
_____

Sources of information

Surnames in Ireland

First Edition, December 2000

* Seven hundred surnames

* Gaelic form

* English variants

* Septs

* Branches

* Territory of origin

* Distribution in Ireland

* Estimated number of bearers

* Frequency in England and Wales

* Frequency in Scotland

* Frequency in United States

ISBN 1 871509 39 4

$15.95 *post free*
seanquinn@donegal.net

From Seán E. Quinn, 57 Glenoughty Close, Letterkenny, Co. Donegal, Ireland.